Clubhouse Culture

Compiled by
Pete Cohen

First published in Australia in 2021
by KMD Books
Waikiki, WA 6169

Edited by Tracey Regan
Interior design by Dylan Ingram & Chelsea Wilcox

A catalogue record for this work is available from the National Library of Australia

National Library of Australia Catalogue-in-Publication data:
Clubhouse Culture/Pete Cohen

ISBN: 978-0-6451669-2-7
(Paperback)

ISBN: 978-0-6451669-3-4
(eBook)

INTRODUCTION

Thank you so much for purchasing *Clubhouse Culture*. It was such a great expereince putting it together. I want to thank everyone we interviewed, who openly shared their stories and wisdom in using the Clubhouse app.

I want to say a massive thank you to Karen McDermot and the team at KMD Books. They have poured everything into this project and given all their time and support. We have collaborated so that all the proceeds of the book go to support Coco's Foundation. For the past eleven years, Coco's Foundation have been helping improve the lives of orphan children like Xolani in some of the poorest parts of Africa by providing food, clothes and shelter.

I would like to give everyone who purchases this book a special gift by giving you access to my 30 Day Kick Start Programme.

www.mi365.me

Change your life in 30 days!
I'll Show You, Step By Step, How To Take The Lead In Your Life, Feel Extraordinary And Take Hold Of Life's Boundless Opportunities.
Learn how to build massive momentum towards your goals, install the habits of highly effective people and make success and achievement an everyday part of your life.
Let me guide, coach and support you. Just give me 30 days and

I'll give you the exact step-by-step method for getting you on your A-game and staying there for 365 days!

Every day you'll have access to a new training session, introducing you to a new idea or concept. By investing the time each day, the programme will build over the 30 days to put you in a powerful place in your life. Change your life in 30 days!

CONTENTS

CONTENTS

Rob Moore
@robmoore

2x Public Speaking World Record Holder | 💡 The Disruptive Entrepreneur™ | 📈 Investor | 🎤 Speaker | 🎧 Podcaster | 📖 18x Business Author Inc. Best-sellers 'Money', 'Life Leverage' & new book 'Opportunity' | 👤 I help entrepreneurs start & scale their business & create multiple streams of income

WHY ARE YOU ON CLUBHOUSE?

I'm in a syndicate mastermind and a few of our members were talking about Clubhouse and saying that it was an interesting new social media platform. It was at a time where I'd freed up some space, as I had operationally retired from our training companies last year. Had I still been involved in those companies, I probably wouldn't have made the time to check it out, but because I was liberated time-wise, there were about seven of us who looked into it together. (Now the UK Mod Squad).

As is often the experience, I was a day or two in and kind of hooked! I love audio anyway and with nearly six years into my podcast, audio format works for me.

WHAT IS YOUR STORY?

So, I have an eight-figure a year property and business training company in the UK. I've been doing that since 2007. I've written eighteen business books, my most recent released in March 2021. I have a podcast called *The Disruptive Entrepreneur,* which has had nearly 650 episodes over the last five years. I'm also a real estate investor/developer, with nearly a thousand units under management within our property companies.

I've been developing and creating content through social media to help scale up entrepreneurs for probably seven or eight years, so if I'm honest, that has likely helped me build a profile a little bit more quickly on Clubhouse. I already have the story and experience, as well as the Rob Moore Foundation, which helps young and underprivileged people start meaningful businesses to change the world.

WHAT HAS CLUBHOUSE DONE FOR YOU OR OTHERS?

Clubhouse has already outgrown all my other social media platforms. Within eleven days it overtook my Twitter, which I've had for six years. Within thirty days, it overtook my LinkedIn, which I've had for nearly twenty years, and within fifty days, it overtook my Facebook, which I've had for nearly ten years. It's on track to overtake all of them combined in a few weeks time, except for my podcast, because that's in the millions.

So from a profile growth perspective, it's been viral and unparalleled. I guess by the time you publish this, I could have a quarter of a million followers or more. In the first sixty days I am approaching 170,000 followers. It's given me significantly more brand exposure globally. The only thing that has done that for me previously is my podcast, which is listened to in 204 countries. About 90% of my books and 95% of my customers are UK-based, so Clubhouse has given me an unprecedented global scale up, and realistically, I would say I've spent an average of four hours a day actively engaged on Clubhouse, giving value, answering questions, offering experience, support, guidance, and content.

It's hard to say what impact that has had, but just to give you an idea, in one of our rooms we had over 46,000 people. That's one room, in one day. We could have reached hundreds of thousands, maybe millions of unique people in just a few weeks. I've had hundreds of direct messages saying how the content is inspiring them or how it's helped them implement strategies in their business to make money or turn things around, or even in some instances, change the direction of their life.

Who knows, it's early days. But the ripple effect could be huge. I'm currently 95th highest following in the world on Clubhouse, which is fantastic, and most of the people above me were in it from the start.

WHAT DOES YOUR FUTURE LOOK LIKE BECAUSE OF CLUBHOUSE?
Well, part of the reason why I've committed four hours a day to Clubhouse, other than the fact that I have the free time to do so, is because quite honestly, I feel I missed the big opportunities with TikTok, Instagram, YouTube, podcasts, and Facebook. I wasn't an early adopter.

One of the reasons I committed to really trying to push as much as I could on Clubhouse, was because I felt finally I might be in at the early adopter stage, where the growth is exponential and where you see a lot of the benefit. If that continues, and hopefully it will, we can impact millions of people across the globe. If that doesn't continue, well, our contingency plan is that roughly 12% of people who follow me on Clubhouse end up following me on Instagram. And already in the first sixty days, we've just surpassed £100,000 in sales directly from Clubhouse without even having an offer or expectation.

Looking at revenue, if we just trickle down through people who show an interest in what we do and set that trajectory, and if that continues with the platform growing to a hundred million users, well obviously, that could be pretty exponential.

I also just enjoy the format. I like helping people. I like the reward of growth while other social media platforms seem to be throttling your reach and punishing your growth. Plus, the collaboration opportunities are endless, which is great, as I've met more people in America in six to eight weeks than I have in eight years on other platforms. I've done all sorts of podcast collaboration episodes and shout-out swaps and am talking about business or product partnerships or exchanging services.

I've been speaking at summits and events, and been interviewed on big podcasts. I've been interviewed on three podcasts that have more than a million followers, so long may that continue.

CLUBHOUSE TOP TIPS

1. Get a good bio written. Give a full but brief CV of your achievements with a little bit of your story, but not too much.

2. Make sure that all your accounts are linked, you can link Twitter and Instagram, and make sure that those platforms are populated, so that when people go to your Instagram, it looks like it's an active account.

3. Jump in as many rooms as possible. Ask as many questions as you can so you can get up on stage. If you do that enough, some people are going to have you involved in the future, so be patient if you don't get on stage straight away. Just keep going into the rooms and listening, you'll get there in the end.

4. When you're on stage, share your strategies, tactics, tips and advice, that way you can grow your own following and start your own rooms. You can start your own rooms on any niche or theme, so I do Money Monday, and I do business and entrepreneur rooms.

5. Make sure you connect with everyone on the back channels. When you're in a room with people, message them on Instagram or Twitter, or if you can, engage with them on WhatsApp, say that you enjoyed sharing the room with them, and it's great to connect. Try and take as many relationships as you can, away from Clubhouse and have phone conversations with people to get to know them and look for collaborations and partnerships and joint ventures, in which you can forge many. And of course, if Clubhouse does die out, or another social media platform sets up a rival feature, if you've got a lot of connections and collaborations, partnerships and friendships because of your time on Clubhouse, it's already justified your time.

Dame Kelly Holmes
@damekellyholmes

🌍 Global Inspirational Speaker | 📺 TV Personality | 📕 Award Winning Author | 🎧 Podcaster | 🏃 Corporate Fitness and Wellbeing Advisior | ☺ Mental Health Awareness Speaker

WHY ARE YOU ON CLUBHOUSE?

I first came across Clubhouse when my friend James said, 'Have you heard of this great app?' I didn't have a clue about it, but I signed up, though at the time, I didn't do anything about it. I felt it was just another social media platform. But then, a few people were going in to have a look and I started to go on, too. And then, of course, I got hooked. It was a fascinating process and conversations you overhear keep you intrigued, so I kept going back.

WHAT IS YOUR STORY?

I'm ex-military - ten years in the military and twelve years as an international multi-medallist athlete, including two-time Olympic champion. I made the move into business as a global international speaker and author. I started a charity in 2008, to assist disadvantaged young people in areas of deprivation with mentoring programs. Currently I have a fitness business, a property business and continue to be a global motivational speaker.

My ultimate dream is to create mentoring programmes for Olympic champions, as well as the Army's physical training structure. There are many ups and downs in sport and when having a focus on a career that's so big and so elitist, it can have a negative impact for different reasons, with an affect on your mental health and wellbeing.

When you're training as an elite athlete, you must focus on a goal. It is so embedded in your DNA to achieve it; you just keep pushing, pushing, pushing and pushing. There was a great deal of disappointment and injury, in an era when no-one talked about mental health awareness.

The effect on your mental health is quite traumatic, and I am publicly known for speaking out about when I had a breakdown. I was clinically depressed and would self-harm. I've had mental health issues on and off since then too.

The last time I self-harmed was in 2017, the day my mother passed away. I realised she didn't have a life to lead, but I do. It gave me a reason to stay strong and focus on who I am and what I've done. It helped me transition into believing more in myself. Of course I have off days, I get pissed off or annoyed, but I'm in control of getting to a point where I am aware if things get overwhelming.

WHAT HAS CLUBHOUSE DONE FOR YOU OR OTHERS?
Clubhouse has been a great way of connecting with people and industries that I'm really interested in when people don't necessarily know me. When I first got into Clubhouse people were talking about imposter syndrome and I thought, 'Oh, they're going to ask me a question or to speak about something, 'because

all of these people seemed to know everything inside out. But I soon realised that unless you put your hand up and open your mouth, you won't get the questions answered, and you won't get the connections you want.

For me, it's given me confidence to go on stage and just ask a question that maybe thousands of people would love to know the answer to, but never get to the platform, because no-one knows them. I've connected with some fantastic entrepreneurs in all different industries; a couple of them have actually become mentors for me. Some of these are people I'd never even heard of, let alone thought I could connect with. It's given me a great platform to bring alive my passions, and to connect with like-minded people, people that are driven to succeed in life, and also people that have failed but are willing to keep getting up and going again. I think it's a strong network of people who are supportive and push you.

WHAT DOES YOUR FUTURE LOOK LIKE BECAUSE OF CLUBHOUSE?
I'd like to be on there a lot more and develop more contacts. As I said, it's so easy to have imposter syndrome when you've come long-term from a particular industry where people know you for one thing. It doesn't get boring, but they do ask the same questions. In Clubhouse, I can go into different rooms outside of what I'm known for, as I believe I've got more to give, for example, from my military background.

Because of the environment I grew up in, I can talk a lot about identity and feeling empowered. I also have a great deal of knowledge around mental health awareness. I have a real love of property and interior design too, which is just a personal thing, but it's something I love to talk about. And then when you go to the realms of trying to get funding from angel investors, this is a completely different language and completely different world, but I believe you learn every time you ask something. Listening in on Clubhouse, you learn something new every day, because there are so many diverse and knowledgeable people.

You can also learn where your skill sets aren't quite there yet. I use the same analogy as I did in the Army and in sport, that if you get the right people around you, you can have the vision, creativity, and be the driver of your life. Get the right people behind you and you will achieve in life. So for me on Clubhouse, it's about having more of the confidence to go out there and be who I am.

As Eddie Izzard says, 'Be unapologetically you. 'I'm a driven person and if I want to achieve my ultimate next goal, whatever that may be, I need to have the best team behind me. I want people around me that see my vision and know I am a winner, and then I will be a winner.

So when using Clubhouse to build more contacts, the people you surround yourself with can also help build your new identity, who you're becoming.

CLUBHOUSE TOP TIPS

1. Be inclusive. One thing I learnt early on was from a moderator who was blind. She couldn't see who was speaking and so asked everyone to introduce themselves each time we spoke, even if we had spoken before. So I introduced myself, and when I finished, I said, 'I'm finished speaking,' and then introduced the next person. I felt that was a nice thing, because it's meant to be inclusive, which is the way we hope the world is going to be. I also found that we're talking very openly on Clubhouse.

2. Discover who you are interacting with. On Clubhouse all interaction is by voice, but we also have the chance to look at their profiles. If they're the people you want to connect with, you can connect outside of Clubhouse on Instagram or through other platforms, and that will build a stronger connection.

3. Give everyone a chance. It's worth remembering that everyone is very different. You could be a multi-award winner or an entrepreneur with just twenty followers, so some people may not give you credibility. However, it may be that it's just their first day on Clubhouse. So I think it's about giving everybody a chance to put their hand up. Have a look at them and see who they are and what they've done, as they might have some really valuable contributions.

4. Don't be afraid to ask questions. Put your hand up and ask a question, as many of the people listening were probably thinking the same question. Let everyone be aware of who you are and this will give you more opportunity. It doesn't always have to be the same people speaking all the time. Be authentic and have a full profile and people will ask, 'Who are you?' Be open about yourself. Try different rooms, there are so many, and you'll get information on things you didn't even know you were interested in.

5. Don't stay in your comfort zone. I try to go into some of the American rooms with people who don't know me because then I can sit a little bit in the background and listen. And if I'm brave enough to put my hand up, they look at my profile and get me up. Then it's a completely new audience. So, you know, go into places that you wouldn't normally go.

Pete Cohen
@petecohen

⭐ HIGH Performance Coach | 🎁 Author of 20 books on personal and professional development | 📣 Motivation Speaker | 🌐 Worked with Ronnie O'Sullivan & Arsenal Football Team | ✅ Founder of Mi365 Coaching | ✅ I coach legacy makers to shift from thinking to being

WHY ARE YOU ON CLUBHOUSE?

I'm on it because I was asked, but I ignored the first invitation. When I was invited, I was like, 'Oh, no, not another app,' because for me, the last social media platform I subscribed to, was Tiktok, and I was thinking, 'I can't. I don't want to talk. It's just not for me. I don't want yet another social media platform.'

So, I just ignored it. But then I heard a few people talking about it and realised that there must be something in it. I must admit I had to hear it maybe fifty times from fifty different people before I decided, 'Okay, I'm going to give this a try.' And since I entered Clubhouse, I basically feel I've been living in a different world.

WHAT IS YOUR STORY?

I've been in the business of personal professional development since 1989. I first became a fitness instructor, aerobics instructor and personal trainer. Prior to that, I had a terrible time at school. I was diagnosed with severe dyslexia and attention deficit disorder. I hated reading and didn't read my first book until I was thirteen.

But, it's amazing how things change, because I've now written twenty books!

Some of those have been bestselling books around the world, published by Random House HarperCollins. I was on television for a number of years when social media really kicked off with the video element of it. First it was Twitter with Periscope. I did that right in the beginning; then Facebook, then Instagram. I really enjoyed all of that but felt there was something missing. It's very one-way and one-way is still good, but there's nothing like communication. Really great communication is always two-way or multi-way, because when you're hearing from lots of different people, you get lots of different perspectives.

So, my goal has always been about helping people and coaching people. It's the essence of who I am. I'm a coach; I've worked with Olympic champions and world champions, in fact, we recently had Ronnie O'Sullivan join us on Clubhouse.

I'm also obsessed with solutions. My mum always said there's an answer to everything and my dad's favourite saying is, 'It's not what you know, it's who you know.' So my life's work is simple; find out where people are and find out how they feel about where they are.

If they want to go forward, I find out why they might not be able to, based on their relationship to their past, or their trauma, or their personality. I can help them deal with that before they realise, 'Okay, this is now where you want to go.' There are specific steps. I can either help you get there or if I can't, I'll find someone who can. That's my story.

WHAT HAS CLUBHOUSE DONE FOR YOU OR OTHERS?

It has completely changed everything. It's actually hard to put into words, as words probably won't do it justice. It has given me the opportunity to connect in a way that is beautiful and so impactful that you can feel it. You can feel it when you're hosting a room or listening to people; you feel a connection. So, I crave connection and I crave to be heard, but I also crave to create a space for others to be heard. It's just amazing.

And it's also allowed me to help lots of people, with many people getting into my programs. It's also allowed me to make some fantastic connections, with so many people, even one on one.

I've also created a by-product which I was not chasing at all, but has just happened. It's called 'Talk-ability.' If you want to be successful in life, especially if you have a product or service, you need talk-ability.

So, in Clubhouse, we talk about this in a whole new way, which exists only in our minds. You can go into different rooms and just listen. When you come out of the room, you can reflect. 'I know people are talking about me, they're thinking about me.' In the morning, when we do the room called, 'How to create your fantastic future,' we have people coming in from all over the world. I'm going to start putting pins in a world map I recently purchased so I know exactly where these people are. And we're taking note of every one of these people. We've been doing it for about three weeks now; we know who's coming in, we know what they want, and we want to serve those people as best as we can.

And I promise you, we've only just started with the impact that we're going to have on the world.

WHAT DOES YOUR FUTURE LOOK LIKE BECAUSE OF CLUBHOUSE?

I always wanted to be an actor when I was young, but I really struggled to learn lines. Surprise, surprise. So, the future for me is about taking the stage a lot, but not just for me, I will be bringing people onto the stage for them to be heard. There's going to be more of that.

I also want to show you that I'm a big fan of magic wands. I have a picture of me somewhere from when I was four years old, holding a magic wand and I want to imagine a magic wand in my hand whenever I present. This recently connected when I learnt what abracadabra means. Someone in Clubhouse came in and told me that it comes from the Hebrew words 'I create as I speak.' That just blew me away, it connected to my future of giving people the opportunity to create more by speaking more.

And that's how this book came about. An idea came to me, that I'd love to do a book about Clubhouse. I only had to think it, and then say it out loud. Then I spoke to my publisher, Karen McDermott, and before she could even think about it, she said, 'Yes.'

It's magic and we're going to get this magic out into the world.

Many people will read these stories from inspirational people, whose words will touch their hearts, in the hope that they too will be inspired to create their own stories. The future is inspirational, not just for me, but for everyone.

CLUBHOUSE TOP TIPS

1. Know why you're using it, otherwise you could just get lost in it.

2. Be curious, really curious about what people are thinking and doing. Go into lots of different rooms. I mean, you might hear some very strange things, but curiosity is such an important virtue.

3. Raise your hand, get up and speak. Public speaking is a big fear for many people, but the way to overcome it is to get more comfortable doing it.

4. Sort out your bio. When you see pictures of me, you see a duck on my head and one of the moderators said to me the other day, 'I don't understand why the duck is on your head, can you explain that in your bio?' So, get your bio right.

5. You want to make the connections, so make sure you have something to offer people, that it's attractive and it's appealing in your bio. Collaborate with people, make friends, and take some of those connections off Clubhouse. Meet them on Zoom so you can see their face, or even in person, if you can.

Karen McDermott
@karenmcd

✏️ Author of 40 books | 📚 Publisher of over 400 | ✖️ TEDx Speaker | 👶 Mum of 6 | 📣 I operate 3 small publishing presses & a publishing academy for self-publishers

WHY ARE YOU ON CLUBHOUSE?

Clubhouse came onto my radar back in January 2021. I think people had been on the platform for a few weeks before I got in there. I was curious. I am curious by nature so I went in to quietly check out what it was all about and started exploring, just going silently into rooms. But when people from Australia knew me, I didn't get to just slip silently in and I ended up on stage. It was interesting that I didn't get to stay in the audience for long. What captivated me was how openly people shared their stories and how people helped each other. My whole purpose in life is to help people share their stories with the world and it wasn't long before I answered the call and offered to help Pete bring this book to life.

WHAT IS YOUR STORY?

I'm based in Perth, Western Australia, originally from Ireland and I've been here for thirteen years. Before I came to Australia, I had worked in mental health for four years. Then I became a special needs tutor, as well as becoming a teenage mum at nineteen.

I always ended up as the boss in any job that I got because I have leadership qualities and a can-do attitude. Ten years later, I went back to university and studied humanities. I had a dark period in my life, when I went through post-traumatic stress and a double miscarriage. It kind of shook me up a bit, I went inwards and did the work I needed to become a butterfly. I call it my cocoon period.

During this time, my husband and I made the decision to apply for residency in Australia, which took two years to happen, but when it did, it was divine timing. I haven't stopped since we moved to Australia. I was thirty-five weeks pregnant with my third child when my feet touched the soil here. I started to write and I started to write children's books for my kids because, you know, there's spiders that can kill you and snakes and things that we don't have in Ireland. So, I started writing about those kinds of things and we created children's books around our kitchen table. We called them Mamma Macs' Homemade Children's Books and Mamma Macs is actually a real character that maybe you'll see sometime. She made an appearance recently on the Duchess of York's Storytime with Fergie and Friends.

About two years after I emigrated I had just had my fourth child. She was four weeks old and I got the call to write a novel and in the novel was going to be woven my miscarriage story and the epiphany I got that was gifted through watching *The View* and listening to Whoopie Goldberg one day. She shared with a reality TV couple that their miscarriage was a visitor that came to tell them that they need to get back on the right track in life and then their gift will come. So, I wrote that novel in thirty days and somebody read it and said it was the answer their heart longed for.

So, I got it published but it was a negative experience. It was a heart-centred book but it didn't feel like it when I held it in my hand. But the quote at the beginning of that book is, 'From every negative situation is the potential for a positive outcome.' And I turned it around. With a bit of research, I discovered that the printing and distribution channel my American publisher had used, had just opened an office in Melbourne, Australia.

I applied what I learnt from that experience to become a publisher and I've been publishing for others and myself ever since.

WHAT HAS CLUBHOUSE DONE FOR YOU OR OTHERS?

I love the whole Clubhouse concept. Now I'm a TED Circle host, I find there is a similarity there because Ted Circles do not broadcast the inner circle conversations, they are private conversations in a safe space where people actually open up more and it's facilitated by somebody who hosts that circle. The power is in the coming together of diverse minds who offer alternative perspectives. So coming into Clubhouse, I see it as a similar platform but it's more accessible. You don't have to apply and register. I adore that you can just go freely into rooms and listen.

And I adore that there are people showing up and giving so freely in there. It's a safe space for people to open up. There are some rooms though that I don't like. I'm not into some of the very intense rooms. I don't go for that. But that's okay, you know, other people like that. So that's for them.

I'm actually not on Clubhouse as much as I probably should be because work is busy, but when I pop in there's always a conversation happening. I commit to the rooms that I know I really enjoy and I often do it on a Sunday.

WHAT DOES YOUR FUTURE LOOK LIKE BECAUSE OF CLUBHOUSE?
For me and Clubhouse, I like to give value. So I intend to jump in, create some valuable content for people, maybe make some of my own rooms and share some of my programs. I have a strategy to bring in authors, make them visible, and get the conversation started to facilitate some advancing ideas, you know, that really educate authors. And also people who want to share their stories.

CLUBHOUSE TOP TIPS

1. If you're new to it and going into some of the smaller rooms, do expect to be pulled up on stage or asked to join the conversation.

2. Have a quick intro ready so that whenever you're on stage introducing yourself, you have it down to about forty seconds, that's enough.

3. Give value. Clubhouse is a giving platform, so whenever you go in to give, you will still receive and people will respond to you.

4. Expect people to direct message you on Instagram. I get a lot of messages and I always make sure that I answer them as quickly as possible and help people out. But if you're really popular and you're getting a lot of DMs, I would suggest limiting replies to a timeslot of about fifteen minutes.

5. Keep your boundaries in there, you can still be giving, but be strategic in being able to identify who needs the help, rather than who is just connecting for the sake of it.

Glenn Marsden
@glennmarsden

🎙 Mentor | 📈 Entrepreneur | 🔊 Public Speaker | 🎧 Podcaster 'ImperfectlyPerfect' | ⭐ Interviewed 350+ International Public Figures | 🗃 Exceeded touching the lives of over 10,000 people in the last 8 months running workshops throughout Australia, New Zealand, the USA and the UK

WHY ARE YOU ON CLUBHOUSE?

I heard about Clubhouse predominantly through the business network on LinkedIn. I heard people talking about it and it was getting bigger and bigger.

I'm across all nine social media platforms, creating initiatives and posting every day. I don't follow the algorithm because I'm trying to cater towards each individual, and I make sure I go against it. So when everyone was talking about the app, I was pretty much like, 'Oh, I got another one.'

But after a couple of days on Clubhouse, I really took to it because the thing I like about it is that it's auditory. It's taken the visuals away. You have to really listen intently and other than looking at someone's bio, there's no pre-judgement, you're just listening to somebody speak. That's what I actually like. I think humanity has come around full circle during COVID-19 and it's making people pay attention and actually listen to a person rather than looking at a person. If you're watching something, something happens in your mind where you can look at it, but not really pay attention. I think there's something truly magical in the auditory medium. When people are talking and it's just audio, you have to pay attention. It's fascinating.

WHAT IS YOUR STORY?

I'm the founder and CEO of the Imperfectly Perfect campaign. I'm a consultant whereby I help companies and individuals grow their business through marketing, branding and gaining exposure.

Six or seven years ago, I turned thirty and was working in the health and fitness industry. If you could hear my accent, you'd know I'm very British, but I've been living in Australia for seventeen years. When I turned thirty, I suddenly found I was comparing myself to people and it developed into a lot more than that – I developed body dysmorphia.

I was looking in the mirror and seeing what I thought were my perceived flaws. I couldn't look the way I thought I wanted to. I mean, on Bondi Beach, I was seeing people who looked like they just walked off a catwalk or out of a magazine. I wasn't as naïve to think that they may not be taking additional supplements, but when you hang around with these people and they're saying they're not and you're kind of doing the same exercises, and you're eating the same, it starts playing with your head.

Well, I started looking in the mirror for three to four minutes, and after a while I noticed it was getting to be three to four hours. While living in Sydney, Australia, my wife and I had our first child and if you know anything about Sydney, it's really hard to get child care. So, at the time, we decided we would move either back to the UK or go to Thailand.

Because of the British weather, we chose Thailand, but living in a new culture without my friends, without everything, I found myself going down the rabbit hole to a worse place than ever before. I found myself making excuses to go to the bathroom just to check myself out in the mirror whenever we were out.

It got to such a bad point that I hid away for about seven months, but my wife was picking up on it. It got to the point where she sat down one day and said, 'It's taking you away from me, it's taking you away from our newborn. You have to get help or we're going to go our separate ways.'

So, I broke down; it was the first time as a guy, I actually cried. We went to see a GP in Thailand, but because it was all in my head, he couldn't find anything physically wrong. That was when I realised I had body dysmorphia. I know, because I Googled it; I defined it myself.

Moving forward by the grace of God, we got a call to say we could get child care five days a week in Sydney, and I was able to find work there. So, I thought my prayers had been answered, we moved back to Sydney, things went back to 'normal,' and I felt a little bit better.

However, it was still there. I went to see somebody about this thing I had created. The first time I saw a psychologist, they were trying to pertain it to something from a past childhood trauma. It wasn't, so quite frankly, I got frustrated but I kept on training and kept on going. One of the trainers in the gym suggested I speak to a psychologist who specialised in cognitive behavioural therapy, and he was able to help me get things into perspective.

Being in the health and fitness industry, and with a knowledge of sport science, I know the make-up and physiology of the body, but what you see in the mirror compared to what is in your head can be two different things. It showed me how strong the mind can be as your demise. That's why I'm so passionate about mental health.

Things improved a lot from there, but two years ago, I realised in retrospect, that a lot of what I was doing was comparing myself on social media, when I found out an old friend in the UK had taken his life. When I saw his child in a video, it really hit me as a father. I cannot imagine having to say to a child that their father is not coming back. I became passionate about wanting to bring awareness to mental health and body dysmorphia and empower others who are struggling. So I reached out to some organisations, but obviously there are plenty of mental health advocates out there, so I didn't get far.

But then I thought about reaching out to public figures, and working on a campaign with them, because we all look up to the screen, or athletes and corporate leaders, and think they have the perfect life, but they still have the same struggles. I'm also pretty good with photography; I'm able to capture someone's life energy and their essence.

So within three months, the Imperfectly Perfect campaign got picked up by the media. Within six months it was in many publications. In twelve months we've been featured in over 100 publications and networks around the world, America, Asia and the UK.

WHAT HAS CLUBHOUSE DONE FOR YOU OR OTHERS?

The first couple of weeks I was on Clubhouse, because I'm very much one of those people who gets quickly into things, I was in audiences and chatting straight away. Behind the scenes in my business, I researched how to do press releases, media clicks, and learnt how to network the right way by picking up the phone. I just knew that my project was far bigger than my ego and I had to get comfortable with feeling uncomfortable.

So when Clubhouse came on, I jumped in. I loved the aspect of it being auditory because no-one is judged on their professional appearance. People come for a commonality. They want to join forces very much like yourself, to bring people together. For me, Clubhouse has been about getting on stage and meeting people.

But it was also intentional because I wanted to get in front of key players to look at partnerships over in the US, as we are now moving towards the corporate sector to disrupt corporate silence. If I can reach the top of the corporate sector, it will create a ripple effect, which will indirectly go through to the employees. Employees will take it to their home life. Then we can finally get kids talking about mental health. That's what changes culture.

Basically, that's why I started in Clubhouse. But what I actually found, as well as connecting with these key players, was I built real, genuine relationships with them. When I go into a room, I'm very much a person who picks up on good vibes and energy.

So if I feel the energy is not right, I'll leave and go into the smaller rooms, where you can have some of the best conversations you will have in your life.

You will meet people from all walks of life who share their vulnerability. That's what I'm about. Showing vulnerability is a sign of strength. And many people I'm speaking to on Clubhouse have said that when they've opened up, it has been better than spending three years in therapy. The oldest form of communication is storytelling, and when people come together and share their stories, it makes us feel less alone.

As long as it's being moderated properly, when I do rooms I've started bringing in people that I know, like a clinical psychologist or a therapist so that people know there's an action point to go to. That's my thing, because in a room if you are talking about mental health, you should have someone there that you can refer people to and watch out for triggers.

WHAT DOES YOUR FUTURE LOOK LIKE BECAUSE OF CLUBHOUSE?
Well, I've started moderating in quite a number of rooms. We've got some rooms coming out where we'll have some CEOs and VPs of corporations over in the US and in the UK who are going to jump onboard with the mental health stuff. And in terms of numbers, I think it's going to open to the public soon, so watch out!

For me, I'm connecting with some incredible people and I'm actually taking it off the application so that I keep those relationships building. As soon as the doors open, I do think some of those opportunities will ease out. At the moment, there are quite a lot of big players who are making so much money and then you've got the groups which are smaller. As time goes on, I think it will even itself out because there's a lot of diversity right now.

CLUBHOUSE TOP TIPS

1. Go in with an open mind. Don't just go in and look for people that you've heard of before.

2. Introduce yourself and jump up on stage, especially if you've got an opinion on the subject. When I facilitate rooms, I tell people although we might just be moderators, we're here to facilitate an open conversation, so everyone's on the same playing field.

3. You can learn from every single person that you meet in all walks of life. Don't look to a particular profession. You're more likely to end up doing a business deal or collaboration with someone you have a shared interest in, rather than somebody that's not even in your industry.

4. Jump in but have no intentions. Well, you can have an intention, but don't have any preconceptions about what you're going into. Just utilise it as a social media app whose sole purpose is to connect people.

Randa Habelrih
@randa.habelrih

♣ Entrepreneurs with Heart club founder | ❤ Connecting heart-centred entrepreneurs looking to align profit with purpose | 🎙 International Award-Winning Speaker | ✏ Author | 🏫 Educator | 🎁 Founder of 2 not-for-profits | 🏢 Real estate investor | ✋ Autism MATES club founder

WHY ARE YOU ON CLUBHOUSE?

I joined Clubhouse when I received an invitation from a friend. At first it looked like spam, and I thought, 'I'm not going to click on that.' Then, I reasoned my friend wouldn't send me a virus. I hadn't yet heard of Clubhouse, but I thought, 'What the hell?'

So, I clicked on it and realised that it was some sort of application. Once I was in I was fascinated. I joined in January, and those first two weeks were bizarre because I was mesmerized.

I was on the app day and night, going in and out of rooms, trying to follow interesting people; all the big names were there and they were running rooms. These guys were spending so much time on the app, I thought there must be something in it. For those first two weeks, that's pretty much all I did, I spent all of my time listening and learning. I really didn't start talking until the end of the second week.

WHAT IS YOUR STORY?

I live in Sydney, Australia, and I'm the CEO and founder of the Autism MATES - it's a not-for-profit that's near and dear to my heart because it was inspired by my son, Richard.

He's an amazing young man on the autism spectrum and he's my pride and joy. Richard has overcome so many obstacles, more than most of us will ever encounter. When he was very young we were told he would never walk or talk, and now he's a paid public speaker. He's just launched his first animation *Timmy the Turtle* at New South Wales Parliament House and at Hoyts. It is inspired by his puppet show, which he takes to schools to educate young children about kindness, inclusion and acceptance of diversity. We've employed other young people on the autism spectrum to be part of the creative team. We plan to establish a social enterprise whereby those young people will collaborate, write and produce the sequels, giving them employment and dignity, a sense of purpose, a sense of belonging, and a sense of achievement.

Following many nasty bullying incidents that Richard experienced, I became an advocate, educating people and school students about autism. I was an anti-bullying campaigner, and I still am because Richard had such an awful time through school. I don't believe children are nasty by nature, they either learn that behaviour or it's just out of ignorance. They have no clue how to interact with children who are different. I guess it's hard enough for kids to fit in at school, so to expect them to go out of their way without giving them tools or knowledge is a big ask. I realised education is the key. So now, I run speaking events and conferences and talk about autism and being different, and I feature autistic speakers so that the humanity behind the diagnosis is presented.

I never expected to be on this journey. My background is in corporate marketing and I loved my role as national marketing manager for a French multinational cosmetics company.

I had to leave my position to look after Richard full-time as soon as he was born, but I also had to replace my income somehow. He had so many issues and anyone who knows anything about special needs parenting knows that your expenses go through the roof. There are things you could never imagine you would have to pay for; speech therapy, occupational therapy, physiotherapy, psychology, specialist paediatricians, testing, IQ testing, all sorts of things. And so I worked out a way to replace my income. I taught myself to trade options and property.

I was able to study and do this from home, which meant I could look after Richard as well. We were doing therapy with him eight hours a day, six days a week. We got him walking and talking; he was initially diagnosed with severe autism. His current diagnosis is level two autism plus he has an intellectual disability, so while he is a public speaker, he's not an eloquent speaker, but he gets his message across and the audience loves him! He loves to play to a crowd and has no fear of the stage.

He's amazing. He brings the room to its feet because he's so authentic. And he's quite a charmer without even realising it. It's just who he is.

WHAT HAS CLUBHOUSE DONE FOR YOU OR OTHERS?

It's opened up a world I never expected. I'm in Australia, and I used to do a lot of travelling pre-COVID, but even when I attended live events overseas, big events, I would only meet a handful of people that I would strike a connection with. Clubhouse has allowed me to actually engage at a much deeper level than I could at any live event and with so many different people from all walks of life.

When people voice their message or tell their story on Clubhouse, you can hear their authenticity and you relate to them. You then invest the time to get to know and connect with them. You might join their room, or invite them to join yours. Clubhouse has opened up the world in real time and it's a fast connector.

There is real authenticity on Clubhouse, because unlike other so-cial media apps, you can't hire a videographer or a copywriter to make you look good. It's instant. It's authentic. It's your voice. It's right here and now and it's not scripted.

I now run two clubs. One is Entrepreneurs With Heart, which has really surprised me. It's hit a nerve and people are enjoying it. They're turning up and we have engaging conversations. The goal with this room is to amplify people's impact. The room tends to attract social impact entrepreneurs, people who want to make a difference in our world. The goal is still to attract people who want to focus on profit for purpose because we need resources to make a real impact. The room unites like-minded people and in-troduces them to people who could assist them in achieving their goal, the moderators share their networks, offer advice and also offer encouragement. The entrepreneurial journey can be isolat-ing, so we also offer accountability and connections with a com-munity. We're looking for people who complement each other. In the first couple of weeks we had relatively small rooms with about twenty or thirty people, then about the third or fourth week we started to lose track of numbers, the room grew, and people kept returning to make connections - that's what happens on Clubhouse.

We had a thirty-six-hour room once, and I closed it because it was exhausting. I did have a sleep and some wonderful moderators kept the room going. The following week we did six-and-a-half hours and last week we did another six hours. I think I've settled into a five to six-hour session.

There's always people who want to speak. And I've even received messages asking why I cut them off when this is a 'room with heart.' But I can't keep going longer than six hours and with the time difference it means I finish up at about midnight my time, so that's my limit.

My second club is Autism MATES and it's an extension of what I do on other social media platforms, that is, I have conversations with other parents and professionals in the autism space. My goal with Autism MATES is to educate and empower. My inspiration is, of course, my son Richard.

WHAT DOES YOUR FUTURE LOOK LIKE BECAUSE OF CLUBHOUSE?

I've connected with amazing people who I now call friends and I hope that the rooms will continue to grow and help amplify the impact and reach of those social entrepreneurs who are doing good in our world. My future because of Clubhouse has increased my reach and impact and I now belong to some amazing communities and have expanded my network exponentially.

I've participated in international conferences and I contribute to other clubs and other rooms as a co-moderator, so I try to give back to those who assist me in running my rooms.

Alone, there's only so much you can do, but when you unite your efforts with like-minded people, that's when you can make a real and sustainable change. You can make an impact. It's not just one lone voice. And that's what Clubhouse is about.

CLUBHOUSE TOP TIPS

1. You've got to have a decent bio. There are some people who just have a couple of lines and then there are others who have pages and you have to keep scrolling. There is such a thing as less is more. The first three lines of your bio are crucial, because that's what people see and then if they're interested, they'll expand. Put in a little bit of humour or something personal to keep it interesting, because people will base their decision on following you, pretty much on your bio.

2. Prepare your introduction. If you're going to put your hand up, especially in the big rooms, if they invite you up and it's a big name, you need to sound confident, professional and polished. So rehearse how you want to introduce yourself. Don't just say, 'Hi, my name's Randa and I'm from Australia.' Practise presenting yourself in the best possible light in a few punchy sentences and ask your question.

3. Be strategic about who you follow. If you follow people who just have a big name and aren't really aligned to what you want to achieve, you're going to be 'unbalanced' and your newsfeed will be filled with their rooms which may not align with your purpose and interests. So choose who you follow very carefully.

4. Engage in the smaller rooms. I often use the big rooms as a podcast – I just listen. I have this rule where I have to start my day at the gym. That's my appointment with myself and I always used to listen to music. I now listen in to the big rooms on Clubhouse, where I'm not likely to be called up. I listen, I learn, and I learn how they run a room. I learn how they cut people off. I learn how they answer people and how they introduce different topics. And I learn from their content and as well as what not to do.

5. Give value. I always I go in there with the intent to give value, whether it's to give advice or to connect or to just support somebody. If somebody's start- ing a room and they say, 'I need help moderating,' I'm there helping them because it's a bit daunting. With your first room, I always advise people to ask someone to moderate so you're not there alone. It's happened to me and that's why I bring someone to moderate. And then as the audience builds up, you're okay.

Dr Pooch
@drpooch

🍉 The Dr. Seuss on Superfoods | ✏️ First NFT children's book Author | 👶 Making holistically health literate youth | 💡 Founder Dr. Pooch Foundation | ⭐ Creator of the Get Well Johnny children's holistic health series

WHY ARE YOU ON CLUBHOUSE?

Well, I was selling a book actually. I was doing a presentation at a store in Los Angeles and I randomly met a woman who bought a couple of my books. I meet a thousand people a day, but I always remember people. She said she was from another state and we exchanged information.

Months and months later, she reached out to me. When somebody texts out of nowhere with an invitation for what she called 'an amazing app' that's in beta mode, and I have never heard about it before, I listen. I'm aware of what I want and actively manifest in my life, so I'm aware of when signs show up to lead me in the right direction. At that time, my android was failing, I had dropped my phone so many times and it was broken on both sides, so I needed a new phone. When she told me the app was on iPhone, but I didn't have one, she said, 'Well, get an iPhone,' and that was my sign. I got an iPhone and the rest is history.

WHAT IS YOUR STORY?

I am a certified holistic health coach, but before that, I was a hip-hop head just doing music. I toured all around the world, with music being my focus, but writing has always been a cornerstone. Writing has always been my passion.

I was born in LA. My father is from West Africa, so he has family kind of spread around in the French diaspora. He sent my brother and I to Paris when I was in sixth grade. I stayed in Paris for nine months and then went to Senegal for four or five years to continue school and just get away from the mess that was going on in the United States and in Los Angeles specifically. When I came back, my parents divorced, and it was a bit messy for a while. I went to college, but I was always in and out because of my experience in a Francophone system. Schooling there is much more advanced than the United States. It gave me a different kind of thinking. I took that mindset into community college, and I took all the writing courses I could. I felt like there was a calling within my pen.

At that time, I was also learning Chinese as I wanted to study to be a Chinese traditional doctor, but the further I studied it, I found it wasn't for me. And so I guess I was on a path of merging these two worlds of health and writing. And it all came together around 2011, 2012, when I came up with what is now called the *Get Well Johnny* book series. There are twelve books, with what I think are the twelve most important topics we can introduce to children to initiate them into the world of holistic health. These twelve books literally give them the tools they need to stay healthy and maintain health throughout their life. They'll be able to diagnose the ailments of their parents, literally no joke. With most doctors only studying nutrition for around thirty minutes during their coursework, reading my book series will give children more knowledge in holistic health than most doctors!

With childhood obesity occurring in one in three children nationwide in the US, and every inflammatory and chronic disease increasing, this is a systemic problem that no-one is talking about, that is directly impacting our children. A couple of the books in this series are *Super Foods are Super Fun* and *Water Is Life,* educating kids on some of the most important issues affecting health.

WHAT HAS CLUBHOUSE DONE FOR YOU OR OTHERS?

It continues to bless me. My first conversation on Clubhouse was, literally, amazing. It has opened me up to a whole new world. It's so powerful that we're talking right now, and we've developed a kinship. It's allowed me to connect with inspiring people who are mentoring me.

I'm also mentoring them; we're exchanging services, something that is really important. There's one guy in particular who mentors doctors. He helps doctors to scale their businesses and he's mentoring me. But I'm giving him value too, in consultation that's specific for him.

I'm able to be of service and others are being of service to me; everybody wins. And some people will pay for services.

Clubhouse has, kind of, put a fire under me too. It's shown me my work is important, and I'm not delusional about what I do. I'm very aware of the impact I have and who I am as a person, but it just reminds me that I have to actively be out there talking about these things, talking to people, and continuing these conversations. Being in these groups has encouraged me to have my own podcast so I can continually put the message out into the ether, out into the cosmos, and people can respond.

There are parents out there right now, who are just a little bit aware of the toxins that are everywhere, and they have to be careful what to buy. I want to magnify that so we as consumers can decide what we buy for our children. It's already changing how corporations are interacting with the public. With my work, I see my books as the first step, but there needs to be a children's holistic health marketplace where we know that what we are giving to our children is healthy and toxin-free, creating a whole generation of healthier kids.

Some people are sharks, they're targeting kids to capture them for life. We're going to do the same thing, but putting in nothing but good; encouraging holistic values, meditating and encouraging millions of children to have a better connection with food. And then who will their kids become? Just like somebody who grew up in the '70s is teaching their kids through Dr. Seuss in the '80s and '90s, so it will magnify.

That's change at a fundamental level. Everything is changing. So I'm thinking super big. It could be that it won't happen in my lifetime, but everything has to start somewhere.

CLUBHOUSE TOP TIPS

I like to think of Clubhouse like this: I came into this new year wanting to change my set of friends. I said, 'If my friends are broke, I'm broke. Right. If I'm hanging around millionaires, then I'm the next millionaire. Which is it that I want to be?'

So, whatever you want to become, then you have to hang around people like that. When I'm listening in different rooms to different motivations, different coaches and millionaires, people that are at the head of their field doing what they're doing, different doctors, it's crazy the different levels that I vibrate on.

So, I'm treating this like it's casual, I'm tricking my mind that all these amazing conversations are just a casual conversation between a friend and I. And as these people are my friends, they're here to support me. Even if I'm not chiming in or I can't raise my hand to come in and talk, I'm still invited to the party. I'm in there and this is my realm of influence now.

That's my top tip on how you treat this. You can create your own life. You can create and tailor your experience to hang around whichever rooms you choose. That's what you want to vibrate on at this point. Whatever you are looking for, there's a room for that. I choose the rooms I want to spend my time in.

You can create this like you were at high school; you can pick and choose your friends. Even if you don't say anything, you're just in the room, you're going to get the vibration of what those people are saying. Your mind is going to start saying, 'Oh, I'm accepted here.' And once you're accepted there, you're a part of it, and then you start changing yourself into whoever you want to become.

That's how I'm using Clubhouse. I took the opportunity to join with my new phone, and I didn't even swap my numbers. I didn't add my old contacts. The people that I connect with daily are all genuine people that I want to stay connected with, otherwise they're not going to be in my phone. These new connections that I'm building are encouraging my creative endeavors. I'm not stuck in my old patterns, specifically not having money or not doing the things I want to do.

And I don't want the money for me. I want it to be able to do things that have meaning; to create the change I seek in holistic health. So, this new me is hanging out with you now and hanging out with millionaires and influencers, which is the beauty of it.

Whatever you're into, you can find what you're looking for in Clubhouse, and feel like you've been invited to the party. After all, we just want to know we have friends out there and we are accepted.

Hip-hop taught me that I have a voice so people can feel inspired. Step one is my books, but I have to continue just pouring this out into the world. Just like the legacy that is Clubhouse. It is a voice for all of us. And it's 'no strings attached!' It's a place where we all can connect and come together.

Ryan Nurse
@ryannurse_

👋 Quit my day job because of Clubhouse | ⭐ Traumatic brain injury survivor | ☀ Overcame depression | ⭐ Founder 'Myself' | 👻 Life Coach & Inspirational Speaker

WHY ARE YOU ON CLUBHOUSE?

I joined Clubhouse to provide value to others by sharing my story and the life lessons I have learned. To listen, learn, support, and serve.

WHAT IS YOUR STORY?

I'm from Buckinghamshire, south-east England, and I am a traumatic brain injury survivor and thriver who has also suffered from and overcome depression.

In 2011, I was attacked on the way home from a nightclub. With no physical signs of trauma I went home as usual. After my parents failed to wake me the next morning, I was rushed to hospital for an emergency brain operation. I suffered from a fractured skull, and a blood clot due to a bleed on the brain.

I was put into an induced coma and my parents were told I'd be lucky to survive the night. Three days in, specialists planned to switch off my life support machine as there was zero brain activity. However, my dad saved my life by refusing to turn the machine off.

The first time they reduced the sedation to bring me round I wasn't breathing so had to be put back into the coma. The following day was my final chance. Thankfully, I did respond, however, a specialist told my parents *IF* I was to ever wake up, I would never walk or talk again and would be in a vegetative state for the rest of my life.

Whilst in a coma I had an out-of-body experience where I viewed myself through the eyes of my creator. From what I witnessed, I believe I was sent back to finish the job I was put on this earth to do. The first time I realized I was awake and alive was very surreal, especially in an ICU alone looking down at the tubes and needles penetrating my body.

I did have to learn to walk and talk again, and the first time I walked myself to the toilet on my Zimmer frame was the day I realised how lucky I was to be alive. I remember washing my hands and the feeling of someone staring at me. As I slowly looked up my eyes made contact with this 'thing' that was staring back at me, and I was left with a feeling of utter dismay. The second time I looked up I was scared, as I didn't understand what I was looking at; staples down its head, hole in its throat, eye pointing upwards and a face like a skeleton. *Frankenstein* was the thought that came to mind. I cried after realizing it was me.

Over the next week I focused on improving my walking and talking, to the point I was transferred to a hospital closer to home. After two days in the second hospital, I was told one morning that I could go home. My parents did not believe me and had to confirm with the doctors. I remember that late November evening walking out of the hospital on crutches, stopping in the car park and me and my parents grabbed each other, 'You're coming home,' they said.

I was out of hospital in under a month and was told by the surgeon I was a walking miracle.

Soon after, I met a woman who is now my ex-partner. She introduced me to world travel, and we went on multiple trips per year over the course of the six-and-a-half years we were together. After returning home from Florida in late 2018, she told me we should stop spending as much time with each other. I was gutted and didn't know what to do with myself. Although we were still living together in separate rooms, she wanted space. The more space I gave her, the further we drifted apart.

After spending Christmas and my birthday alone, I plucked up the courage to embark on the trip we had planned for Cape Town in March. The weekend before I left, after struggling to book a table in every local restaurant but one, I ended up bumping into my ex (who wanted to be single) with another guy. As much as I was heartbroken, it was also a huge sense of liberation.

On this trip I felt like a completely new man, but upon returning to an empty home, the depression really kicked in. I was desperate for external happiness and ended up resorting to drink and drugs. Contemplating suicide through months of mental misery, one single thought transformed my life, 'Could I live with the thought of dying with regrets?' I soon realized the nightmare I was going through was a dream for someone else. By practising daily gratitude, I felt like I had become a positivity magnet. Before you know it I had a release date from the prison I was trapped in, which some people call a home.

I set myself a travel goal to visit a different country every month for a year, but this was stopped due to COVID-19. Seeing many people suffering during these difficult times, I asked myself how can I help others from my journey. I became vulnerable and started to share my story online and discovered that this is my purpose. I started to write my book titled *Could I live with the thought of dying with regrets?*

After connecting with Ajay Gupta via Clubhouse, he challenged me to quit my job to follow my mission. I knew deep down that this is my calling and I had to take uncomfortable action. One week later I did. If it wasn't for Clubhouse I wouldn't have. I had to take the leap and hope the net appeared and if it didn't, I would soon have to learn how to swim. With no income and no clue what to do I felt uncomfortable. You must remember that your comfort zone is where your dreams go to die. In life, if we don't sacrifice for what we want, then what we want becomes the sacrifice. Surely if the WHY is strong enough, the HOW will reveal itself …

WHAT HAS CLUBHOUSE DONE FOR YOU OR OTHERS?

Clubhouse has been an absolute blessing, as I have been drifting through life for many years with no sense of clarity or direction. However, through the power of Clubhouse, I have managed to network with some phenomenal individuals who have helped me discover my true hidden potential.

WHAT DOES YOUR FUTURE LOOK LIKE BECAUSE OF CLUBHOUSE?

My future on Clubhouse is looking extremely compelling because it will continue to allow me to learn from and network with many incredible individuals, which in return will help me accomplish my life mission.

I've been speaking at summits and events, and been interviewed on big podcasts. I am now spreading my message globally and creating a future to positively impact the world.

CLUBHOUSE TOP TIPS

1. Be authentic - People want to hear the true imperfectly perfect version you, so just know that it's okay for you to be you. For a long time I would try and get everything perfect until Pete told me to start speaking from my heart rather than my head. Vulnerability is a superpower.

2. Provide value - Be interested rather than interesting. Go into Clubhouse with a 'what can I give' attitude, rather than 'what can I get' and that way you will receive more than you could ever imagine.

3. Don't be afraid to ask questions - Raise your hand as soon as you enter a room. You may not get up on stage, however, if and when you do, make sure you have a question to ask even if you already know the answer. Know that the only 'stupid question' is the question unasked.

4. Respect the room - Listen to the rules of the room and respect everyone who is in it. If the room says no sales pitching then don't try to sell your products or services. Respect that everyone is entitled to their own opinions. You don't have to agree and if you don't like it you can always 'leave quietly.'

5. Show up - Consistency is key. If you frequently show up and follow the steps above you will be noticed and doors will begin to open for you

Namelokai Sein Kina
@namelokaisein

Ceo Of The New Lioness Fire Llc | Trauma Informed | Survivor of Female Genital Mutilation | Keep Girls Safe Foundation President | John Maxwell Trained | Mom of 2 Young Adult Lionesses & 1 Teen/Lion | Leo Manifesting Generator | Kenyan by Birth | US Citizen by Choice

WHY ARE YOU ON CLUBHOUSE?

A friend of mine posted about Clubhouse on Facebook in December. I am a very curious person, and as she started describing what Clubhouse was about, that it was only for people with an iPhone, and invitation-only, I was interested. I asked her to send me an invite, though she said she only had two because she was new. It wasn't until January that she was able to get an invite for me.

However, I didn't know how it worked and couldn't find anything interesting, so I got out. But then a lady from the UK connected with me on Instagram after she went through Clubhouse and saw my bio. I hadn't even written much – it was a tiny bio. She told me she wanted to know more about female genital mutilation and wondered if I could teach her. She told me she believed her mum is a survivor but would never speak about it.

We just connected; we had a two-hour conversation. Before moving to the UK, she was raised in the United States and didn't understand the cultural differences or have much of a connection with her family in Africa. I know how she feels as I have raised my children in the US and know that it's a completely different culture. I am lucky to take my children back to Kenya during the summer months, but not everyone has that luxury – I'm lucky I get to travel to Africa with my work, so I only have to pay for tickets for my kids.

Anyway, she wanted me to join her on Clubhouse. She told me it was a place to connect with many people to get my message out there. She said, 'You're doing an amazing job, and you're writing a book, there'll be so many people willing to help you, as you're non-profit, and you'll be able to grow.'

… And so, I got into Clubhouse, but I wasn't ready to talk. I knew I needed to start telling my story and being authentic. Still, I got into trouble a little as I wasn't careful which rooms I was going into, but then I found myself in Pete Cohen's room, and the love I received was fantastic, and now I have so many followers.

WHAT IS YOUR STORY?

I am a lioness and survivor of female genital mutilation. I don't want to share my story from a place of pain. I want to share from a place of power and a place of peace. The reason I share my story from a strength perspective is because I am a warrior, I am not a victim. I'm a victor. I survived. I know girls who died from female genital mutilation, girls that were my friends. I stayed so that I can tell my story. Yes, I may have been through a lot of pain in my life, but I want to tell my story from a place of hope.

The World Health Organization classifies female genital mutilation as the alteration of the female vulva for non-medical reasons. There are four different types of female genital mutilation; Type I) removing all or part of the clitoris; Type II) removing all or part of the clitoris and the inner labia; Type III) narrowing the vaginal opening by cutting and repositioning the labia; and Type IV) any other harmful procedure done to the female genitals for non-medical reasons.

I was between the age of eleven and thirteen (I can't remember exactly as I've blocked a lot out) when I went through Type I, and my life was never the same again. I remember kicking the women, telling them to leave me alone, spare my sisters, and not go through with it. The women didn't listen to me. They went on and did it. I just remember passing out. I found myself in bed. I bled so much, and I got an infection, but I healed, thankfully. God saved me so that I can be a voice against this awful rite of passage.

Instead of them teaching us as girls how to be good teenagers, how to go to school or learn how to get our periods, right after mutilation, we were forced to marry someone who is often thirty years older. It's usually someone who already has four or five wives – you might be number five or six, but we still didn't get taught anything about having a husband or being someone's wife.

Women are considered property, and we are lower than anything; girls are only there to be seen and not heard but let me tell you something, I have fought my way out, and I have survived and continue to beat the odds. I told my husband that I was going to school; as my grandfather told me, education is the only thing that can give you back your voice. In middle school, the headmistress was so mean to me because I was a teen mum. She told me several times I was stupid, and I would never see a college door. She even called us prostitutes. Those words got into my heart. I believed every single one of them. And I gave up, and I never worked hard in school. I graduated with the lowest points to go to high school. When I went to high school, I failed with a D+ because I believed those words.

When I came to the United States, I met a man in a community college in Wichita, Kansas who was kind and encouraging. When I told him I wanted to go back to school, he helped with the placement exam and mentored me into believing I could do it. I told him how I had failed high school and how the words from the headmistress had hurt me. This was the first time I was validated and was inspired to use those ugly words as inspiration to beat the odds. I reminded myself those words every time I wanted to give up.

On top of that, I was diagnosed with dyslexia, but I did not let it stop me. I kept pushing because I wanted to prove to the people who called me stupid that I was not stupid. I worked so hard that I graduated magna cum laude with two bachelor's and a master's degree, though if you ask me how I did it, I wouldn't be able to tell you.

I was living in a relationship with domestic violence, but I was so scared of leaving because of my children. I did not want my children to be a statistic; most African Americans who move to the US don't have fathers at home. I wanted my children to have a father, so I continued to stay in the pain of humiliation every day; I was beaten up and physically, emotionally, psychologically and sexually abused by my husband. I was a walking corpse.

But then, one day, I found my voice, and I will never let anybody take my voice away again. I finally divorced him; when I left, I was 305 pounds. But I like to say I lost 145 pounds of pain and suffering and gained freedom, love, light, and peace.

That's who you see right now. I am a lioness, unstoppable and unapologetic. I got my voice back. I didn't get it back easily, but freedom is now given, freedom is taken, and that's what I did.

WHAT HAS CLUBHOUSE DONE FOR YOU OR OTHERS?

Clubhouse has validated me. When I met Pete, he showed me that he didn't care what I looked like or where I came from, but he told me, 'I see you. I hear you, and you matter.'

Do you understand what those words mean to me? I wasn't seen or heard for so many years, but a stranger telling me those words means 'life' to me. And then someone else saw me, invited me on stage to speak on Clubhouse and I told my story. This one moderator told the guy who was running the room that I had it listed in my bio that I'm writing my book and looking for money to help publish the book. These strangers came together and raised $3,100 that I used to pay an editor who is currently editing my book. Since joining Clubhouse, I have received unconditional love and I don't want Clubhouse to ever change. My life has changed for the better due to Clubhouse and I am so grateful

WHAT DOES YOUR FUTURE LOOK LIKE BECAUSE OF CLUBHOUSE?
The future for Clubhouse and me is to continue making authentic connections with people and to continue being a voice for women and men who feel like nobody sees them or hears them. I want to be that voice. I want to be that light. I want to be that love. I want to grow my club and my tribe. I want to show those who are suffering from PTSD like me that we can get through it. I did it. I got out of a dark hole, and you can do it too.

That's my Clubhouse future; I want to build a huge family.

If you would like to support my efforts, please visit: www.keepgirlssafe.org

CLUBHOUSE TOP TIPS

1. Be authentic; be unapologetically you. Don't feel judged; just say what you need to say. You never know who is listening. Sometimes you are in the right place at the right time. Don't question the universe.

2. Take the excellent advice you hear and put it into the entire operation. I've only been on Clubhouse for a month, but I've learned so much. I'm doing Pete Cohen's thirty-day challenge, and I was just telling people in his group that I had never seen myself the way I see myself now after taking the class. I don't go to bed without doing the sixteen-minute meditation. I do it twice a day, in the morning and the night. I've already sent it to my two daughters. There are people from all over the world who genuinely want to help people.

3. Don't go onto Clubhouse to sell anything. Go in there to give and receive. When you are prepared to give, you'll find so many doors start to open for you.

4. Monitor your time at Clubhouse. Like all social media, Clubhouse can be addictive. So, consider your self-care. Go for a massage or just take some time for yourself ... don't spend all your time there; make time for self-love, as I say, 'If I don't love me, I can not love anyone else.'

Peace Mitchell
@peacem

💜 Co-founder 'The Women's Business School' | 🏆 Winner 2021 PauseFest Superconnector Award | ❌ TEDx Speaker | 🥇 Co-founder 'AusMumpreneur Awards' | 📕 Author of Amazon #1 best-seller 'Back Yourself' | ✅ Forbes Business Expert | 🛩️ Australian Ambassador of Women in Tech Global movement | 🐍 Women's Entrepreneurship Day WEDO Ambassador | 🎤 International Speaker | 🧒🧒 Mother of four amazing humans | 🌍 Host of Women Changing the World at Clubhouse

WHY ARE YOU ON CLUBHOUSE?

I discovered Clubhouse on 1 January 2021, which is so interesting because my word for the year of 2021 is CONNECTION. I realised I'd set the intention for connection and the next thing I knew, Clubhouse came along.

I've connected with so many interesting people from all over the world and it's been an amazing journey so far.

WHAT IS YOUR STORY?

I'm co-founder of AusMumpreneur and The Women's Business School. I have an online community of fifty thousand incredible women, and we connect experienced entrepreneurs with those just starting out. I've had my business for twelve years and I'm based in Australia in a tiny little rural town called Innisfail. When we started our business there was no-one else locally running an online business, and when we told local people what we did, they thought we were talking about our imaginary friends when we said we had customers on the Internet.

I love what I do. I'm really passionate about working with women and supporting them to follow their dreams in entrepreneurship.

I trained as a primary school teacher at university, and when I had my first son I realised that I had to choose whether I wanted to be at home or be in the classroom. I remember ringing the school and saying, 'Can I just teach school of the air?' Like, why? Why do I have to be physically in the classroom? Is there any way I could be at home? And there wasn't.

I was told I could do part-time or 'something different.' I think it was probably around that time I realised if I wanted to have flexibility and time with my baby, I needed to have an online business. But it has taken a really long time to get to where I am now, which is running my own school.

I now have The Women's Business School and I'm back teaching again, which I love and I'm working with women in entrepreneurship. It's quite different from my days as a primary school teacher. Business is such an incredible journey. I think you learn so much about yourself, as well as personal development and overcoming self-doubt and fears. There are incredible challenges you have to overcome as a business owner. It's such an interesting journey and not for the faint-hearted, that's for sure. It's certainly not the easy option, and life would have been much easier to work out some child care arrangements and keep teaching in the primary school.

But I love what I do. It just lights me up. I've had so many incredible experiences and met so many amazing people as a result of having my business.

Our vision for The Women's Business School is to be a global business that empowers women, and for them to elevate and change the world. I believe that the number one way to change the world is to invest in women because we see the world differently. Women have different perspectives on solutions to problems. They have unique and creative ideas. And they approach life differently to men.

Men and women are different. Women bring a different perspective to the way they do things and the drive behind a lot of women is not just about the profit. Of course they want to be profitable, but there's a deeper purpose behind what they do. That's what gets me excited. I want to work with women who are on a mission to change the world in big or small ways.

WHAT HAS CLUBHOUSE DONE FOR YOU OR OTHERS?

Clubhouse, for me, is all about connection and the relationships you build. It's quite incredible that the people you meet and are attracted to are found just through reading people's bios. You can get a sense of who they are and then go onto Instagram and see whether you're aligned to someone.

That's really interesting to me because shared values are really important, for any interaction, relationship, collaboration, partnership or someone you want to work with. And it's interesting how the conversations you typically have on Clubhouse are very authentic. There's something about the fact they're not recorded. People are honest and vulnerable and share things they haven't shared elsewhere. I've talked about things on Clubhouse that I haven't talked about on any other social media platforms and I certainly wouldn't write on my Facebook page or put on Instagram.

These things I feel I can talk about because it's a different kind of a platform. It's a safe space in one sense.

WHAT DOES YOUR FUTURE LOOK LIKE BECAUSE OF CLUBHOUSE?
I've just launched my first club, Women Changing the World, and my vision is to create a community of women who are changing the world. Later this year, we are launching The Women Changing the World awards and I feel like Clubhouse is an incredible way to identify and find the women who are out in the world doing big things. Sometimes they're the unsung heroes, you know, and I'm looking for that magic. I'm searching for those people doing unique and amazing things, and I'm finding them all the time on Clubhouse.

CLUBHOUSE TOP TIPS

1. Reciprocity. The law of reciprocity is that when you are kind to others that kindness comes back to you. I think it's really important to be generous on Clubhouse. Sometimes I volunteer to be a moderator and don't say anything through the conversation. I let the speakers come up to the stage and let the person who's hosting do the speaking. My job is to invite others and to help see what's happening in the room and select people from their bios. It's not always about being front and centre and having the microphone. Sometimes your role is doing other things, and I think it's important to let other people speak, but also to have your turn to speak because reciprocity is all about giving as well as receiving. So, if someone invites you to be a moderator, then it's really nice for you to return the favour and invite them to be a moderator when you're holding an event too.

2. Resonance. Resonance is all about your energy. When you put out positive energy you attract positive experiences, opportunities and connections to you, so it's essential that you make sure you have positive energy when you're going onto the platform because people pick up on those vibes. I heard a tip from someone the other day, they said whenever they're on Clubhouse, even though no one can see you, they always smile and that comes through in their voice and how they're speaking. The other part to resonance though, is protecting your energy, because I found that within a few weeks I was starting to get addicted to Clubhouse. It was so exciting and fun and I got such a buzz from being on it, the people talking and incredible conversations. And I just overdid it. I was on there all the time and I had to take a step back and say, 'Okay, no more Clubhouse. I'm just going to have a break for a few days and then we'll come back to it and I'll be selective with what I'm doing and the time I'm allocating to this platform.'

3. Intention. Be intentional about why you're there. It's easy to waste hours and hours on it, jumping between different rooms. Be intentional about the kind of conversations you want to be part of and the rooms you want to be in. And if you find yourself in a room where you're not enjoying the energy, you don't have to stay. You're welcome to hop out of that room. It's also important to be intentional about the kind of rooms you're a part of and the people that you're connecting with. Really pay attention to that energy. The other thing with intention is having clarity on your mission and vision and why you want to use Clubhouse. What are you there for? What's the purpose? Is it just to have fun or is this a business strategy for you? Getting clear on your intention for participation will help you be intentional with your time on Clubhouse. Be strategic and choose rooms that align with you so you don't waste time. Make sure you are strategic around how you use your time there. Be open. Everyone has a story and sometimes people surprise you, so let them.

Sabrina Stocker
@sabrinastocker

👑 Queen of Personal PR | 🎤 International speaker | 🎾 Tennis Player Turned Serial Entrepreneur | 📺 Finalist of BBC One The Apprentice | 🗺️ Geek at heart, MBA in Strategic Planning | 💃 Salsa Dancer | 🤸 Adventure Finder | 🧗 Thrill Seeker

WHAT IS YOUR STORY?

From tennis player to Forbes featured entrepreneur, it's been a ride! After reaching the Final Five on BBC One *The Apprentice* show, I've been fortunate enough to attend red carpet events, drink wine at Number 10 Downing Street and travel the world, but it didn't start like that.

Growing up was fraught with difficulty. Both my parents were teachers, and money was scarce. They were both phenomenal parents; and invested everything into my brother and I, opening up as many opportunities as possible. I was that geeky kid in school who scored straight A's, and didn't fit in with the other kids.

My love for business started when I was nine years old, watching *The Apprentice* religiously every Wednesday night. I told myself that I was going to win when I was older. At fourteen, I started my first 'business' selling sweets and even hustled my way into selling in my local supermarkets. After that, I became obsessed with learning about business and growth and started watching videos by Tony Robbins and Brendan Burchard around productivity and growth mindset every night before bed.

Fast forward a few years, I was rejected from the University of Oxford and jetted off to Florida. After playing tennis out in the heat for six months, I came back and started coaching and created my first company - My Tennis Events. While working full-time and starting my company, I found a loophole in the MBA administration system and was accepted onto their program without a degree. With running a business, doing my MBA part-time and keeping a busy and active lifestyle, it was no wonder something was going to hit me harder than I could imagine and appreciate, till this happened.

You know when something so life-changing happens, you hear people say that they are glad they went through it? This isn't something I would wish upon my worst enemy. I was driving back from work when my eye started throbbing. I pulled over. Twenty-four hours later, I was in the hospital, speaking to a doctor who was telling me I had contracted an eye infection with a 60% chance of losing my sight permanently. I read the pain I was experiencing was one of the most painful experiences a human can bear. I was unable to sleep for ten days due to eye drops being needed every thirty minutes. I remember at one point, the pain was so bad, I was crying on the kitchen floor with a knife pressing hard into my stomach and trying to commit suicide, but my tennis player mentality kicked in and I knew I was a fighter.

Facebook is a playful thing. I was scrolling down my newsfeed and saw a competition to win a worldwide trip for content creators for a well-known travel agency. I'd applied a few weeks back. As I was rushed to hospital on the verge of suicide again due to the pain, I received a phone call saying I had won the competition. What insane timing! A twenty-one-year-old girl's dream! I had to go. I couldn't let an infection stop me.

The doctor in the eye hospital said if I travelled, I'd almost definitely lose my sight. I wasn't taking that as an answer. Now, maybe it was from listening to all of those mindset videos from Tony from the age of fourteen, or perhaps I knew I was destined for something bigger than myself, but my energy changed.

I can't describe what happened, but something inside me awakened, and I knew I would go on that trip. After that, I visualised every day having my vision back, excuse the pun. And fast forwards six weeks of powerful visualisation and challenging my physical body, my sight came back, and I travelled the world. I scuba-dived and skydived over the Great Barrier Reef, zip-lined the Rockies, and danced on the beach in the Fijian Islands. It was incredible.

When arriving back in the UK, a fire ignited within me and everything was clear. Within six months, I scaled my tennis agency to be the largest within the UK, partnered with corporate brands and federations. I graduated as the youngest person to receive a distinction in my MBA, became a finalist within the BBC One show *The Apprentice,* and was invited to wine at Number 10 Downing Street, plus a spiral of red carpet events, VC and Angel networking meetings, and dinners - life was good.

On 1 January 2020, I remember writing a post on my Instagram saying, 'Challenge me 2020, I dare you.' Oh, what a caption.

When lockdown hit, I lost my agency overnight, living in a flat on my own after breaking up with my boyfriend and I couldn't see anyone else. But honestly, it didn't faze me too much, to quote Heraclitus, 'The only constant in life is change.' There was nothing I could do about the situation. I believe that we have complete control over the way we adapt to situations, and it's within our internal power and energy to control our perception of life.

During lockdown, I co-founded Shopping Slot, a service that allowed someone to type their postcode in and find all of the local shopping slots available in their area. We hit 100,000 unique visits overnight using a viral press strategy, and within six weeks 500,000 users and three million page views within six weeks of launching. We helped hundreds of thousands of people get food delivered. Crazy.

The success of our PR strategy accelerated the growth of Two Comma PR. And it's been incredible. We have worked with thousands of thought leaders on their public relations strategies using earned and organic media placements to get them in the largest top publications, TV, Radio, and number one bestsellers.

What's next? My mission is to inspire others to live their best lives through entrepreneurship. Everything I do is so that the fourteen-year-old girl version of me would have had the option to watch a successful female taking the stage and inspiring her to do the same.

If you feel like you resonated with this, were inspired, or want to become part of this journey, I encourage you to reach out right now to my LinkedIn & Instagram (@sabrinastocker.r). My DMs are open, and I love speaking to action takers to see how I can help or how we can work together.

WHAT HAS CLUBHOUSE DONE FOR YOU OR OTHERS?

Clubhouse has allowed me to have a new family. A family of other like-minded entrepreneurs, ambitious individuals, and incredible people who have come together in a way you would never imagine is possible.

I've been able to open up and talk like I do with my close friends, nurture relationships off the app, and even met up with some Clubhouse friends when travelling in the States!

Podpreneur Alex Chisnall and I, friends from many years ago, created *The Alex & Sabrina Show,* bringing a hint of flirtiness and banter between us, we launched our daily brunch show, with thirty minutes of speed networking followed by a power hour daily at 10am and 6pm GMT. With over 100,000 people visiting our room, we have grown an incredible community and are now launching our podcast.

The Alex and Sabrina Show is creating a phenomenal community. Along with some other incredible co-hosts like Pete Cohen, Lynsey Suzanne, Jose Ucar, Elliot Kay, Jeannette Linfoot, Rebecca Haw, Jeremy Jacobs, and Harriet JW, we are showing up, creating a difference, and opening up possibilities.

WHAT DOES YOUR FUTURE LOOK LIKE BECAUSE OF CLUBHOUSE?

We are growing *The Alex and Sabrina Show* family! We're launching our podcast, community groups, and MasterMind, which I'm incredibly excited about!

There has been a compounding effect from Clubhouse and exponential growth in so many different areas of my life. Within Two Comma PR, we've been able to connect with incredible entrepreneurs who are looking to share their stories and partnered with the most inspiring talent as our clients.

CLUBHOUSE TOP TIPS

1. When opening a room, you are responsible for setting the energy. Let everyone know the format, how the flow will work, and start to create a buzz! You make the environment and allow people to feel comfortable, relaxed, and understand the play.

2. Remember to welcome speakers with warmth, thank them for attending and give them a chance to speak. Speakers and moderators are giving up their time to support you. You want to make sure they have the opportunity to speak, contribute, and feel appreciated.

3. Have clarity in your title and stay on point. Whether your topic is around marketing, dating, or crypto, new audience members are there to listen and only see the title in their corridor. As the host, it is your responsibility to keep the room focused on the topic and, to an extent, allow the conversation to flow in a way that will serve its audience.

4. Create connections offline! Connect with your moderators and audience on other social media platforms, spark a conversation and see how you can help each other out. You never know where the conversation will lead!

5. Have fun with it! Who do you remember the most? The onex who make you smile, feel at ease, and create stimulating conversation. Life's a playground, have fun!

Jan Santos
@jansantos

© Branding & Identity Coach 'The Creative Scoop' | ◎ Entrepreneur
| 🎙 Host of TheCreativeTalkPodcast

WHY ARE YOU ON CLUBHOUSE?

Clubhouse was introduced to me by my friend and mentor, Mary, from Australia. She told me lots of stories of how Clubhouse will revolutionise social media and really connect people, but it's by nomination or invitation-only, and only open for Apple users. I don't use an iPhone, so I took some time, wondering if buying an Apple product was really worth the investment. But I ended up getting an Apple and when I joined Clubhouse the first room I entered was run by Pete Cohen, so it really was a game-changer.

WHAT IS YOUR STORY?

I'm a branding coach and I run a branding agency in the Philippines, with clients in Germany, Australia and the UK. Essentially, I'm an artist. I took a fine arts major in advertising so I focus on that. At that time I was geared towards art and advertising, and then I studied multimedia arts which has given me the opportunity to work in one of the biggest networks here in the Philippines.

The funny thing is, I started at the bottom … back when cameras had wires that people had to hold - that was me. All my degrees didn't matter because that was my first job. And then I was given an opportunity to be a video editor as well as a role in graphics and so I slowly climbed up the ladder.

When I opened the branding agency, it was a roller coaster ride. I flew to different countries, meeting a lot of people, taking a lot of jobs related and not related to my passion and my expertise. But I had a vision that someday I would find the identity that God intended for me. And that's in terms of art, design and branding, though it wasn't clear back then. But fast forward, the branding agency is connecting people; people working with me, full-time partners from different parts of the world.

WHAT HAS CLUBHOUSE DONE FOR YOU OR OTHERS?
Clubhouse has changed the game for me. I love listening to podcasts. I love creating content for podcasts, so Clubhouse gave me a feeling of listening to audio content, but you can also participate if you want to share something. And that's great.

So I started as a listener. I just listened to people, but the conversation connects and it pulls me in so I can talk and share something.

There are two great things that Clubhouse gave me. First, it connected me to great human beings; it started authentic friendships. You feel that you've known these people for so long, even though you just met them a short time ago, that's the feeling I have. It's authentic.

And then on the business side, it's given me a wide reach of connection. There are people that need what I offer who can collaborate with me. That means more stability for the business and you can't find that on other platforms. You may achieve the same goal, but not in the same duration.

You can change your business in a single room. If you connect to people, you can find clients and partners. It's amazing. As of now, I think Clubhouse is the only platform that can achieve that.

WHAT DOES YOUR FUTURE LOOK LIKE BECAUSE OF CLUBHOUSE?
Clubhouse is connected to my vision to reach out and connect, and not just for business. God has been blessing me on all sides - I'm not even looking for clients but there is an overflow of clients and projects. Clubhouse, for me, in simple words, is just talking and listening. I can see Clubhouse as an element, a weapon, if you may, to send out light, giving encouragement and words of wisdom, sharing inspiration. That is the power of Clubhouse.

CLUBHOUSE TOP TIPS

1. Don't start a room immediately. Invest some time to learn the ropes. There are a lot of rookies and newbies just like me and once they get into Clubhouse, they want to start a room immediately. That's not how it works. My tip is to join rooms and not big rooms. Don't make rooms for yourself straight away. Don't be a moderator just yet. There's nothing wrong if you want to participate in big rooms, but in small rooms you will have ample time to speak and the moderator would have more authority and power to extend the time so you can have a good dialogue. And when that happens, people will know who you are and what you do and what you can offer in business or life. A connection and a relationship will be built. And with that, trust will follow.

2. When you do speak, be natural and authentic. Don't throw in a pitch, just start a dialogue and connect and you will be amazed.

3. Be aware of how you use Clubhouse. If you want to say something, you need to be direct and to the point, because Clubhouse is still in its early stages. If you want to say something and the moderator gives you time to speak, you need to maximise that time and be direct.

4. Understand that at the moment the features are limited but very powerful.

Tony Wyles QGM
@tonywyles

🌍 Global Project Manager | 💣 Eradicating Explosive leftovers of War |
♻️ Everyone is needed to reach the Sustainable Development Goals | 🎯
Enabling the safe return of land to communities from explosive devices |
⭐ Helping empower other lives with optimism and a can-do spirit

WHY ARE YOU ON CLUBHOUSE?

The Clubhouse experience for me initially was all about curiosity. I was intrigued to see what all the hype was really about. I am a people watcher, and I enjoy watching the world move about, so Clubhouse had the potential of filling that void during the lockdown.

WHAT IS YOUR STORY?

My journey through life, thus far, has seen certain emotional moments, but nevertheless, I've always identified my profession as a lifestyle rather than a job. In recent times I came across an article by Marc Anthony, the American singer-songwriter, who said that 'If you do what you love, you'll never work a day in your life.' That really resonates with me - I love what I do. The satisfaction of seeing another person's happiness has always driven me to go that extra mile in applying my abilities to help solve their circumstance.

I recently started to question myself and went through some

soul-searching to ascertain my inner me, and why I do what I do, I doubted who I really am. It wasn't long before I found what I was looking for; I'm a humble guy with a beautiful family, my wife and three children. I'm passionate about giving back to others and have been privileged to be active in explosive ordnance disposal and the removal of explosive remnants of war dangers across twenty-five countries whilst gaining countless gratitude and empathy in so many diverse lives and cultures.

I've experienced some pretty horrific things. The nature of bomb disposal, mine clearance and risk mitigation of explosive remnants of war has taken me to some dangerous and hazardous places. I've seen injuries, malnutrition and death. It seems that I was often unfortunate to be in the wrong place at the wrong time, just doing my profession. During the seven years working on and off in Lebanon, I survived being held hostage three times at gunpoint by the local freedom fighter organisation. Ranging from only a few hours to the longest being eight hours, it's quite an experience to go through when you've got a gun pointed at your chest.

During a project in Kosovo in 2000, I was en-route to a small village to eradicate some explosive submunitions responsible for taking the lives of several children and adults when I was taken hostage by the Serbian special police at gunpoint. I can assure you that was probably one of, if not the scariest, moment of my life; they pulled us out of the Land Rover and marched me down to a small stream, whilst constantly screaming at us, pushing and shoving, and telling us that they were going to kill us. They threw me in the boot of a car, and drove us across the border, where I spent the following forty-eight hours going through a good cop, bad cop routine. I even went to court and was fined 100 Deutsch-marks (about sixty quid) for being classed illegal in the country they took us to.

Another time in Lebanon, I was tasked with a rapid response where a team of searchers had been damaged clearing a mine area. After several hours their extraction was completed. I went back the next day to where twelve of us had been conducting an investigation, intending to finish the United Nations report. As I approached the area, I sat my team down for a break and continued forward alone, following the safe lane to the end of the cleared area, when I noticed two blue wires hanging out of the ground within a previously clear part. As I turned to walk away, somebody was sitting waiting for me in a nearby tree and triggered the detonation, which blew me up. That point forward started a new world of pain for me. I was determined though, and after a four-month recuperation, I returned back to Lebanon and then on to another overseas project and continued.

I came back to the UK in 2010 for a routine operation on my stump. I had reached a point where walking was problematic, and the pain was real. The procedure typically should have only been around sixty minutes. However, I took six hours to get out of recovery, due to being overdosed on morphine, although at the time I had no idea what was happening, which was fine - I recovered. Subsequently the next day I became very ill, and instantly was in a critical situation, almost dying again due to a blood clot. So long story short, in five days, I had three general anaesthetics and nearly died a couple of times.

Nevertheless, I have never perceived myself as being in discomfort or having traumatic concerns. I persistently have an outlook that it's just another life chapter. My passions and drive remain to support and mentor others with a notion that can help them create happiness in their lives.

WHAT HAS CLUBHOUSE DONE FOR YOU OR OTHERS?

In late September 2019, I decided to spend more time with my family. I sought to start a new career at home in the UK. Unfortunately for me, it was just before the outbreak of COVID-19 when I began formally applying for a new position.

Over 350 applications later, rejection after rejection, although improving with every application, I just couldn't get through the brick wall which had appeared. Unfortunately, I spiralled into a dark place, which made me feel like I had fallen into a tunnel and couldn't see any light at the end, nor a way to climb out.

When I started on Clubhouse, drifting into the different rooms, listening to others, I heard the phrase 'imposter syndrome.' After a bit of research, I discovered that the feeling of something missing that I have had since my days of leaving secondary education had associations with the pattern-mindsets behind the syndrome. Consequently, Clubhouse helped me change my rationale. It was like a switch had just flicked on for me. Through general listening and discussions, I evaluated how I thought of myself, which helped me unlock something inside. Clubhouse has really opened up some great friendships, provoked reflection, and urged a new desire to continue risk mitigation of explosive remnants of war with the addition of inner self-exploration.

WHAT DOES YOUR FUTURE LOOK LIKE BECAUSE OF CLUBHOUSE?
Clubhouse has enabled me to connect and share with others who I would have never met otherwise. Since joining Clubhouse, I have streamlined and enhanced the way I focus on myself, my goals and visualise my future.

CLUBHOUSE TOP TIPS

1. Sit and listen first - you don't always need to speak just for the sake of it.

2. Don't always believe everything you hear.

3. Go and research what you've heard before deciding who to connect with – you don't need to follow everyone.

4. What is your purpose in Clubhouse? Discover what your goals are and work towards those goals.

5. Words are not actions, so be accountable for yourself – take the necessary steps to make things happen.

Karen Darke
@karendarke

🏅 MBE | 🎓 PhD | ✳ Founder Quest79 | 🏆 Paralympic Champion | 🎤 Speaker | 🧗 Explorer | ◎ Performance Coach (MA) | 📕 Author of 3 books | 🔥 Guinness World Record holder for landspeed by armpower | 👁 Focused on sustainable performance, resilience & inner transformation | 🏔 Creator Adventure Mindset coaching programme

WHY ARE YOU ON CLUBHOUSE?

I got into Clubhouse when I was invited by Pete Cohen. I really love the connections I'm forming and am inspired by the people I meet. I'm not sure how much of the interaction is about Clubhouse or as an effect of COVID-19, but it's led us all to being in a community that's open, honest and authentic.

WHAT IS YOUR STORY?

I seem to have a connection with gold and magic, which I can definitely relate to in this life. It feels like my passion is about helping both myself and other people turn difficult things into good things, so a form of alchemy is what my life is about. I was paralysed when I was twenty-one, so that's taken my life to a different perspective. I've been a Paralympian for twelve years, and I used to be a geologist studying gold, so whichever way I turn I'm connected to gold, whether it's through geology or winning medals, and now supporting people to find their gold.

After receiving the seventy-ninth medal for Britain in Rio 2016, seventy-nine has become a theme in my life. I've been across seven continents, on nine epic rides, taking different people along with me who are just completely stepping into something crazy for themselves because they've never done anything like it before. They've all been on journeys of discovery, as they either have physical or mental barriers. It's been amazing for me to be with them, because I can see it through their eyes instead of mine, which has been very special.

At the same time, because of Quest 79, people have been doing their own challenges, be it physical or other forms, to inspire people around them and change their lives. It's interesting to see how it's evolving. I'm trying to get the balance between letting it be and working with it. I'm also conscious that I have to look after my own energy with it as well, so I'm watching it grow organically, rather than pushing too hard with it.

As a little overview, Quest 79 is about taking a step out of your comfort zone into something which is not too overwhelming, but seems a bit unachievable in some way. It should be something you're excited about it or passionate about, allowing you to discover something incredible in that journey. The idea is to extend ourselves, and push a little bit further to do something that we might otherwise be too lazy to do.

In the process, we find something special in that journey, not only for ourselves, but when we step up and do something unusual or beyond our 'normal,' it helps us to find what I'm calling 'Inner Gold:' something shiny within us that has perhaps been hidden or become tarnished or lost through life's events. In the process of shining brighter, we inspire those around us. It spreads like a positive virus. I've been inspired by so many people doing their quests and I see the effect they have on their families or their communities. The idea is that it spreads positivity for mental and physical health and gives us the realisation that we are all here with a purpose and have so much to give. When we step up and are brave enough to do something like that, then incredible things unfold.

Just a couple of examples; there was an eleven-year-old boy who decided he would climb seventy-nine peaks in seventy-nine weeks. He didn't even like mountain climbing particularly, so it was a big step. He ended up raising money for a children's charity in Africa and really inspired all of his schoolmates and families in his community.

Another guy decided to run his first marathon and people donated blood because a family member, a young boy, had a rare blood disease. He gathered seventy-nine photographs of different people all donating blood. Someone else is planting seventy-nine trees, another is doing seventy-nine random acts of kindness, another, seventy-nine days of litter picking and many other fantastic quests that connect to finding more 'gold' within, around us, or in our environment.

I'm also writing a kid's book with some of the kids' stories that have evolved from this.

WHAT HAS CLUBHOUSE DONE FOR YOU OR OTHERS?

It's been an amazing place to connect with some incredible people, with lots of support from Pete and all the people he's got on board. The whole idea of a quest and a journey of discovery has created connection with so many people. It's been a privilege to meet this community of people and some of the great people in Clubhouse. It's an interesting forum.

It feels amazing in so many ways, but I still feel like I have to protect my energy as I like to be present with the people and places around me and not online too much. I'm amazed that some people are on it so much, like hours everyday, but it's really quite a special, incredible place. There are just beautiful stories of people stepping beyond anything they may have done before.

I've also come across a childhood friend on Clubhouse; I didn't even know until we chatted offline. At the end of the conversation, I said, 'By the way, where are you from? Your accent is familiar.' And it turned out her parents were really good friends with my parents. My parents actually lived in the house she was born and grew up in, and our parents drank together in the 'club' in the village. It seems synergistic that we met on Clubhouse! Rachel is now an energy healer and she did seventy-nine healings in seventy-nine hours on the seventy-ninth day of the year. A beautiful quest, and we have now joined together to take Quest 79 further and wider. We are creating inspiration and events to help raise the level of positive emotions and sense of happiness and wellbeing for all those taking part; to bring out more of the gold we all have inside, to help nurture connections in communities and around the world, and to help protect and have more compassion for our environment too.

WHAT DOES YOUR FUTURE LOOK LIKE BECAUSE OF CLUBHOUSE?
I've actually not been going on it as much lately. I've merged my two rooms into one, but I enjoy the people I meet there and the meaningful conversation and collaborations it leads to. I also

like supporting other people in their rooms, perhaps more than running my own. So we'll see how it unfolds. I think it will continue to be part of my life as I have met some really special people there.

It's an incredible tool as I've never been a person to 'deliberately network.' I really enjoy being social with unusual people and it feels like Clubhouse is full of them. It's surprising how it feels in the right rooms with people who are genuine and open and sharing their souls. It is fascinating.

CLUBHOUSE TOP TIPS

1. Use it in a way that feels right for you. There are some rooms that may throw you off-balance because it's not the place for you, so just find the rooms that feel comfortable, then you can get chatting to the people in there.

2. I think you can find your tribe in Clubhouse, but you might need to move around a bit to find them.

Alex Flynn
@alexflynn01

🚴 Adventurer | ⏵ Looking to be the first with Parkinson's disease to climb Mount Everest | ✖ TEDx Speaker - have spoken in 30+ countries to heads of state, diplomats, CEOs, management teams around the world. | 🎬 Producer | 🎧 Podcaster 'Alex Flynn: The Big P & Me!' | ✒ Writer

WHY ARE YOU ON CLUBHOUSE?

I've had Parkinson's disease since I was thirty-six and I've gotten to a point where I need to achieve something truly epic before I can't. With Parkinson's, I effectively have a time limit. It gives you rigidity and takes you away from things like speaking, walking, talking, sex, and countless other things that most people take for granted.

I joined Clubhouse because I thought, 'Here's an open forum that allows you to be yourself, share your story, and connect with people far better than on LinkedIn or Facebook.' It's a place where you can actually bare your soul and people will listen and connect on a more human and conscious level. And I think that's important nowadays. Hopefully I can find the funding I want for my challenges on Clubhouse.

WHAT IS YOUR STORY?

I grew up in a really great family, but my father was an alcoholic. He was verbally, and sometimes physically, abusive. Every single day he told me that I would never amount to anything. I carried that chip on my shoulder for many years, even after my dad died when I was fourteen. But I thought to myself, 'You know, I'm going to make something of myself one day.' Eventually I fell into the law and became a lawyer.

I had one of those incredible stellar careers that just went from zero to hero in about ten seconds flat. I became general counsel of a multinational and reached the top of the heap before I got diagnosed with Parkinson's. And I thought, 'What the hell am I going to do?' Admittedly, I was in a funk for a number of months and I don't know how I pulled myself out of it. I think it was mostly my kids' influence. I realised that if I didn't help myself, I couldn't help them, and if I couldn't help them, I couldn't help others.

I was already lined up to run the Marathon des Sables; a 150-mile footrace across the Sahara Desert, and I managed to do part of that before being pulled out because of a heart infection. Getting lost in the desert was interesting. When I came back, I sat in my mum's kitchen and my mate, Rich, asked what I was going to do.

I had raised £1,500 for Parkinson's UK, but I said, 'I'm going raise a million pounds.' He said, 'How are you going to do that?' and I said, 'Okay, I'll do a million metres at a pound a metre,' ... I'm a maths genius. And he said, 'You can do better than that, it's only about 620 miles.' 'Alright,' I said, 'times it by ten, 10 million metres.' And he said, 'Okay, but only the races count.'

Some of the highlights included over that four-year period were running 160 miles across the Bavarian Alps in fifty-two hours with an-hour-and-a-half sleep. I ran 1,457 miles across Europe and more than 400 miles with a stress fracture on my right tibia. I crossed 3,256 miles across America in thirty-five days using four different disciplines. I was the first guy to do that. I was on BBC TV for two nights and raised awareness of Parkinson's to over 60 million people in less than a month.

So why am I doing this? There are people out there that need help. There are 10 million people in the world that are suffering from Parkinson's, and there is no cure, there's only a way of managing your dissent with the disease. It fucking sucks - excuse my French. But to be honest, there's nothing worse than being told, 'We can't help you, we can only manage your decline.' Great, thanks a bunch, guys. And then you find out the youngest ever diagnosed was a two-year-old boy. That drives me insane. What kind of life would he have?

The world for people with Parkinson's and other neurological diseases keeps getting progressively smaller day after day. I want to be able to show that disability is not a barrier to achieving more than you think you can. I want them to seize the opportunity and mindset to choose to live life by reclaiming their self-worth, their self-confidence, and rejecting social embarrassment; essentially the ability to become productive people in society.

I can only do that by raising money for Parkinson's research, and to do that, I need to create awareness of Parkinson's. So far, I've raised awareness to 170 million households worldwide.

My next challenge is to conquer Everest. I want to put Parkinson's on top of the world, literally. I've crossed two continents, jungles and deserts, but there's nothing bigger than Everest.

WHAT HAS CLUBHOUSE DONE FOR YOU OR OTHERS?

It's opening up connections on a scale never previously encountered. Honestly, the welcoming I've had from people who have heard my story and want to help has been fantastic.

There's a wealth of human kindness out there, the majority are really good. My intention with Clubhouse is that I'll meet the right company or the right person who is brave enough to champion the underdog, somebody who looks upon disability as not having any boundaries, and then we can all be extraordinary.

I think there will be somebody, a company or corporate entity, that wants to have global recognition and the visibility that climbing Everest with Parkinson's will bring. This could be something that will open up the door to getting up Everest, and achieving that would be truly magical.

WHAT DOES YOUR FUTURE LOOK LIKE BECAUSE OF CLUBHOUSE?

I want to change people's perceptions around Parkinson's, and most importantly, to let people with Parkinson's know they can do more than they think they can. Being that I've probably had this for twenty years, I shouldn't be able to do what I do - but I do.

CLUBHOUSE TOP TIPS

1. Get your face around in as many rooms as possible.

2. Put your hand up and come armed with questions.

3. Connect with people.

4. Offer your help to others first.

5. Be socially engaging.

Lisa Spector
@lisaspector

🎹 Piano Ninja | 🐕 Pet Calming Maestro | 🎶 Juilliard alum | After a freak accident in 2017, my 🖐 ended up with 7️⃣ complicated fractures needing 4️⃣ surgeries. 😔 After a diagnosis of CRPS (Complex Regional Pain Syndrome - dubbed the suicide disease), my 1st hand therapist told me I'd never play 🎹 again. I proved her wrong.

WHY ARE YOU ON CLUBHOUSE?

I was resistant to joining Clubhouse at first because I originally thought it was just another social media platform. I don't need to be busier and I don't need to spend more time getting scattered with different things so I neglected it for a while.

Then I got an invitation and decided to join and I was blown away immediately. Why? It's simple. It doesn't take all the preparation time that other social media platforms take to look good, so you can just be your authentic self. At first, I just wanted to connect with other classical musician entrepreneurs, which I have done and previously I've found that very challenging to do in my age demographic outside of Clubhouse.

Because the people I graduated with are not generally in the entrepreneurial world, when I find like-minded entrepreneurs - it's gold. But then I also began to expand my interests to other areas of life, and the people I've connected are amazing. It's literally rocked my world. I just love it.

WHAT IS YOUR STORY?

I grew up on a piano bench. All I did in my childhood was play piano. Everything I've done is involving piano; all I wanted to be was a concert pianist. And in my adult years, I've grown many businesses out of my musical talents. So I call myself a pianopreneur. I've owned a music school. I own a company that creates music for dog anxiety. And now I'm creating online courses, 'The Music Conservatory,' for dedicated adult amateur classical musicians.

I had a huge setback in 2017. My world came crashing down on me when I had a bad fall and ended up with seven fractures in my right hand. I was told by a medical professional that I would never play piano again. I was devastated. I went through 186 hand therapy sessions and other treatments, as well as four surgeries. And so, for two years, I played music with my left hand only.

I'm now playing full concerts with two hands and one hand. And I share my story of resilience and recovery and I call it Left Hand Lemonade.

WHAT HAS CLUBHOUSE DONE FOR YOU OR OTHERS?

For me personally, when I told my story, I almost immediately got a request for a podcast interview, and I really wasn't expecting that. And even though I've done podcasts before, one of the coolest things about that is that I'm now looking outside of what I think is the right outlet for me. I've been invited into podcasts I never would have considered applying for.

I did a podcast guest appearance that was published on Happiness and previously I would have been surprised that I appeal to that audience. So it's really opening up my way of thinking, who I serve and what I represent.

I did an interview where the host interviews 'out of the box' classical musicians. Well, that's what I am but I didn't even know that platform existed. Then that connected me with other classical musicians who are entrepreneurial, so it's just been fascinating. But Clubhouse isn't just all about my music or business, sometimes I go into sound rooms or meditation rooms. I've even connected with dog lovers.

Clubhouse has helped me a lot in my business creating music for dogs with anxiety. Because I worked in the industry for ten years, when I co-founded a company that I left in 2018, people often know me as that business. I'm now rebranding the new company with a new name, so I love that I can connect and talk about my new business. They sign up for their free playlist of music for the dogs.

Clubhouse feels like I'm skipping to the front of the line; I get to skip all the hurdles by just showing up and being myself.

WHAT DOES YOUR FUTURE LOOK LIKE BECAUSE OF CLUBHOUSE?
There are so many unknowns, but it's exciting to be in it early and to see how it's going to transform. I'm just showing up as my authentic self and staying open. To me, the 'unknown' is really worth being there for.

I think Clubhouse is really going to help me get my message out there, in the classical music world. And that's where I've previously struggled in my business, to reach classical music lovers, so that's great. But part of my story is that my recordings and live performances are not just for classical music aficionados; they're for normal people. My mission is to demystify classical music and so demystify classical musicians, we're just people like everyone else. I think it's already helping me get beyond my normal audience, which I've been trying to do for a while now.

My message to everyone out there is that whatever limitations in life you've been given, no-one has the right to tell you what you can and cannot do. No-one knows you. You have complete control of what is happening in your mind. And no-one knows what you can do with your body to bring you joy, whether it's to make music or to dance or to read or to paint or whatever it is, no-one can tell you what you can't do it, whatever the limitation.

I met a guitarist who came to me with tears in his eyes when he saw me playing left-handed, with my other hand in a cast. He told me, 'Lisa, I closed my guitar case ten years ago because I have arthritis in my pinky finger, and I look at you and realise there's no more excuses.'

So I want to reach musicians like that. But it doesn't have to stop at music. By the time you're middle age, many people have setbacks, whether they're emotional or physical. And you can always get through anything that's holding you back.

CLUBHOUSE TOP TIPS

1. Be strategic in deciding who you want to connect with. It can be a total time sink when you just keep searching for rooms, and you can get lost in the endless variety. So be very strategic with who you connect with, what rooms you want to be in, and who to accept offers from. When I joined, I didn't have many followers so I took advantage of some of the cool invitations and connections I made.

2. Don't stick to just one area of interest. There are so many interesting people and so much to learn, not just for business but for your personal interests, so don't limit yourself or narrow it down to one thing.

3. Focus on giving. It's all about giving. How can you serve? How can you serve your audience? Yes, you want to expand your audience, but Clubhouse will do that for you, if you're prepared to give.

4. Show off your authentic self. Clubhouse makes it so easy to do that. No-one knows if it's just you and your cat, and you're in your pyjamas. If I'm invited to play piano ... I do. I engage on Clubhouse in all sorts of ways, though I don't recommend it if you're in your car!

Rhys Thomas
@rhysthomas3

🏉 Former international rugby player | 🎤 Inspirational speaker | 🧡 Mental health advocate | ❤️ Raising awareness around organ donation | ➕ Helping bring about positive change | 🏃 Elite athlete engagement | 🔑 Use my experiences of not dealing with my emotions, feelings and loss of identity that led to self-destructive behaviours, and how I turned my life around!

WHY ARE YOU ON CLUBHOUSE?

I met a guy that wanted to do a documentary for a company called Beyond the White Line. He invited me onto the platform and within the first couple of days I met Pete Cohen, and from there I found myself up on stage quite regularly, and became a moderator. The networking aspect has been fantastic.

WHAT IS YOUR STORY?

I am an ex-international rugby player and played for Wales. I was twenty-nine when I had a massive heart attack and needed a quadruple bypass emergency operation. Two years later I had a machine fitted called a left ventricular pump. I had multiple issues from both operations between 2012 and 2015, and was extremely lucky to survive. When I was put on the heart transplant list, I struggled with my identity and my mental and emotional health. I had a lot of dark times through those years, especially after my second operation.

When I regained my health 2015/2016, I became an alcoholic.

By 2019, my alcoholism was off the rails. But I managed to stop drinking in September 2019 and have been sober for eighteen months. It's been a confronting journey of discovery.

WHAT HAS CLUBHOUSE DONE FOR YOU OR OTHERS?
It's opened doors to people I would never have met, certainly not during lockdown. In fact, if I had been able to network, it would have taken an extremely long period of time to have connected with people I've now met from all different walks of life, business and mental health.

By talking about my feelings and emotions, I ended up in a mental health sector on Clubhouse, and from talking with people about the charities I'm working with, I've been able to meet like-minded people. I'm so grateful to meet people like Pete Cohen who have been super kind and introduced me to lots of people who want to help me create my future. After eighteen months of being clean and sober now, I still wasn't sure where I was heading, but now with Clubhouse, I have a stronger idea of what I want to do to help others.

In the short time I've been on Clubhouse, I've listened to some incredibly inspiring human beings who have made me re-look at the way I address my challenges. Although I was very blessed and had a level head in my sobriety over the past eighteen months, I didn't quite understand how much my story could be viewed as a success story. It's been a journey of resilience, that has taken me through many highs and lows, and I didn't realise it was to be celebrated and could be used as inspiration to help others.

By seeing other people inspired by my story, I realised I could express that even more and gained the confidence to do so.

In terms of my recovery, it's been amazing to meet other people in the mental health sector who also want to help others, whether that be transitioning athletes or people struggling with mental health and wellbeing, or perhaps many other areas of life.

I'm not exactly sure where I'm going but it's definitely opening so many doors to meeting a lot of people I would never have met if it wasn't for Clubhouse.

WHAT DOES YOUR FUTURE LOOK LIKE BECAUSE OF CLUBHOUSE?
Who knows where it's going! In just over two weeks I've met up to thirty incredible people who have been super kind and amazingly helpful with putting me in touch with others who may be able to help shape my future, to believe in myself, to excel and push on to helping others.

I would like to use my story to build a platform that will help others find a voice, or assist athletes to transition into the real world, or just mental health in general. Allowing people to speak up about their issues and find solutions is important to me, and if I can find some prevention strategies before their situation gets to crisis point, then that's where I want to be.

The impact has already been huge. Within a week of Clubhouse I've been on five or six podcasts, I've spoken to about ten others on Zoom and we're working on collaborating together on strategies to assist in all areas of mental health.

CLUBHOUSE TOP TIPS

1. Be yourself, be genuine, and just tell your story. Don't be scared to put your hand up and meet other people. Contact them outside of Clubhouse on Twitter or Instagram.

2. Don't be scared to meet people or connect, as you never know where it will take you.

Samantha Brown
@samanthabrown

🏛 Real estate investor | ◎ Entreprenuer | 💸 Crypto speculator | 🎥 Live video queen | 👶 Single mom | 🛁 Founder of the Bubble Bath Club | 👽 Sci Fi fan

WHY ARE YOU ON CLUBHOUSE?

I first heard of Clubhouse back in November 2020. A friend of mine, who is an online marketing coach in America, had posted on Facebook (until then my preferred social network) that he was looking for an invite. My interest was piqued. It sounded exclusive and new and I thought it had the chance to go viral, and so I began the hunt for my own invite.

Invites were rare back then, and so it took me a few attempts to find an invite. I finally managed to get on in December 2020, over the holiday period. I had missed the boat on pretty much all other social media platforms, by not joining as soon as I heard about them, and so I intentionally joined Clubhouse and started using it as soon as I could. I coach others on getting customers from social media and so I knew it had potential.

WHAT IS YOUR STORY?

I'm from a tiny fishing village on the south coast of England. I'm a single parent and have been running my own business since my son was pretty small, as I needed a way to support us that was also flexible around me being the main caregiver. I am also a property investor and we have a family business that manages a portfolio of several hundred properties.

Prior to the pandemic, my business was a mixture of online courses and agency work. However, when the UK went into lockdown and I started to homeschool my son, I essentially put everything on hold and became a full-time teacher.

I looked on the lockdown as a blessing, as it showed me how much I had been pushing myself previously, and how simply you could live life. I focused on what I could control, like eating well, exercising, and being a terrible but try-hard teacher! Being on my own (albeit with a small child) did start to take its toll, and I found myself in quite a dark place come November/December 2020.

As a natural extrovert, I really missed people. I don't think I was alone in feeling that way. Humans are social, pack animals and are designed to live in groups with lots of interaction. My understanding is that depression and poor mental health overall has risen over the past year.

Global events caused a perfect storm for Clubhouse to explode. People had not seen friends or even family for up to a year. Businesses had shut down. We hadn't been to in-person events. For huggers like me, it was a sad time. Over the holiday period when we were used to spending even more time with friends and family, we were alone at home. And then an app came along that meant you could speak to people across the world. Most people were taking time off from business anyway and so had the time to spend hours and hours each day on this app, talking to people, learning from people and connecting like they used to. We all became addicted, staying up until the early hours of the morning as this legend or that legend joined the room and we could all speak together.

WHAT HAS CLUBHOUSE DONE FOR YOU OR OTHERS?

For me personally, I've reconnected with the world, and I do mean the world. I've always been a real connector and network-er; I'm the person that knows everybody, what Dan Sullivan calls a supernode - a superconductor. So when I came onto Clubhouse, there were a lot of people on the app that I already knew or knew of, and I would find the best person in an industry or the best person that does X, Y or Z, and try to connect with them or just become a superfan of them. I started stalking around Clubhouse and I was able to connect with the absolute crème de la crème of the industry, in marketing, copywriting and business. I was very quickly able to connect with those people due to the conversa-tional and almost one-to-one nature of Clubhouse.

I'm also quite good at getting excited about people and what's happening and I'm able to bring everybody with me. I started talk-ing about Clubhouse all the time on Facebook, and everyone in my network wanted to join. It became like a giant party of all the good people together. We tend to gravitate towards the people who feel how we do and have the same vibe, so all of the good people seem to come together on purpose, on Clubhouse. One thing I really love about the app is that because people are talking to each other, just their voices, no visual distraction, and often you've got head-phones in, it feels like everyone is literally inside your head.

What it's done for me specifically, is massively expand my network, not just in the UK, but across the world, including the US, Malaysia, even Australia, though it's a little harder because of the time zone difference. I've increased my worldwide connections. Prior to Clubhouse, I had students in my programs from thirteen countries and five continents, but I don't think there's a country in the world that's not on Clubhouse and that I haven't now connected with, and I feel like I've got this big friendship network with people I talk to every day. Not only on Clubhouse but we direct message through WhatsApp, Instagram, over Zoom and the phone. I've had calls with people I never thought I'd be in touch with before, like some of the godfathers of internet marketing. The level of access on Clubhouse is unparalleled.

Of course, there's the personal connection and friendship side of things, but I've formed new business partnerships and created new product and services lines just from Clubhouse. My clients and students have also been able to grow their businesses as a direct result of being on Clubhouse, in record time. It's amazing to see.

Before Clubhouse, most people operated from the viewpoint of selling to people, whereas now I've seen a big transition to what we can do together and how we can reach more people. It's really exciting.

WHAT DOES YOUR FUTURE LOOK LIKE BECAUSE OF CLUBHOUSE?
Well, if I could become the face of Clubhouse, my life would be complete! However, I don't think that's ever going to happen. I would love for Clubhouse to continue as it is; a place where people can really connect, at scale. As it grows, I would love to see

the same kind of partnerships happening and people collaborating together, particularly as it expands out to Android users and other people around the world. I will continue on Clubhouse for as long as the app exists, as it's such a great marketing and business building tool. I hope to continue to run the biggest rooms, with the highest calibre of people on stage, all working together.

I don't ever want it to become me setting up a buying type of environment. That's not my game. Never has been. That's why I think I've really struggled with Instagram before, because for me, that feels like I'm talking at you. I like to foster communities within my audience so that they work together as well.

And Clubhouse does that more than any other social media app. For me, I will continue to run rooms that will hopefully bring the best people to the audience, and also discover new talent in the audience as well. That's really important to me.

CLUBHOUSE TOP TIPS

1. Try not to become obsessed with Clubhouse, but if you do, I promise you are not alone. If you are new, listen in on some rooms first and figure out what kind of style you like. There are Q&A rooms, rooms where people just share their stories or where it's more of a discussion or debate. There are loads of different kinds of rooms. There are rooms for business and marketing, which are my favourite. So first of all, go in and just really listen, see what you like and what you think might work for your voice.

2. Follow as many people as possible, but a varied array of people. There are people from different niches, people who are more fun, more serious, people who have different interests - just get following people because then you'll see lots of different rooms. Absolutely, start your own rooms as soon as possible. I've heard people say to wait until you've got 18,000 followers before starting your own room but I disagree. Find people that you've already got a network with, so maybe even just your friends or people that you've done business with before, or some of your customers, and schedule a room and go for it!

3. There may be people who are your competitors, but you could team up with them and run a room on a topic because you all know different things about your niche. You can easily run a question and answer room. All you have to do is pick a focused title like 'How to do X in your business' and then have four or five panel members that do the same or a similar thing, and invite the audience to ask you questions, because everybody loves a chance to get on stage. Give others a chance to answer questions as well as yourself and over time you will find your voice. You'll realise that you know more than you thought you did and might very well be an expert in your niche! And you might find yourself getting some new clients really quickly. If you think about it, the moment somebody is up on a stage, the consensus is that someone has put them on the stage. Therefore, the speaker must know what they're talking about, even if it's only you that's put yourself up there. The moment you're on a stage, everybody thinks you're an expert. They're going to listen to what you're talking about and they're going to actually believe in what you're saying. It's a really easy way to do business on purpose. You can be speaking and controlling the environment as quickly as possible.

Mayah Riaz
@mayahriaz

👓 Celebrity Manager & PR-to-the-Stars | ⭐ Publicity Coach | Founder of Social Media Kindness Day (in memory of Caroline Flack and supported by Meghan Markle) | ☕ Constantly fuelled by Black Coffee | ✈️ Registered Travel Agent

WHY ARE YOU ON CLUBHOUSE?

A close friend of mine was on Clubhouse, and she said it was a great app. Everyone was telling me about it for weeks, but I thought I didn't need another social media platform as I'm not very active on my social media. But as she isn't on social media a lot but enjoyed it, it intrigued me. So she invited me to the app. All my friends know I love voice notes and so it made sense an audio-based app would be just my bag. As soon as I started using it, I found it was! I loved it instantly.

Clubhouse is like podcasts combined with talkback radio - I love the instant and live element of it; it's amazing. I soon found I was addicted, listening in until three in the morning. I'd go into the American rooms, then in the mornings join in the UK rooms. I loved the live element of it, connecting with your voice is so much better than text, obviously. I then realised how much I could use this app to spread the word about my kindness work as well as teaching entrepreneurs how they can do their own PR. On top of that, it is a great app for making friends and connections.

WHAT IS YOUR STORY?

I'm in celebrity management and a publicity coach. I look after personalities from the world of business, TV and showbiz. I also teach entrepreneurs how to be famous through the power of PR.

As well as the PR work I do, I'm also the founder of Social Media Kindness Day, which was set up in the memory of Caroline Flack. After Caroline passed away, it made me reflect on the industry I was in. But as well as that, I started a new business that, due to COVID-19, was all online. Having been online myself, I experienced firsthand the trolling and negativity, but also saw why my clients weren't putting themselves out there - and it was due to other people's views. I've always said what other people think of us is never any of our business. But that doesn't always help someone looking to go online for business or personal purposes.

So rather than expect negativity and trolling online, I wanted to make it a better place for all. Especially as COVID-19 meant we were all spending a lot of time online whether to work, network, socialise or use as a form as escapism. I also heard stories from parents who got in touch with me to tell me that their daughters took their own life. After their death, they went into their child's messages on social media and saw how their peers had sent messages telling them to take their own life. This isn't just one parent who told me this but a handful. A handful too many. This is tragic. How is this being allowed to happen?

I run a business, I have a membership site. If any one of my members were receiving horrible messages or, God forbid, messages telling them to take their own life, I would have stepped in immediately. Why aren't social media companies taking the same responsibility for what is happening on their own sites?

In order for Caroline's legacy to live on, I set up Social Media Kindness Day, which is on 9 November every year - her birthday. It is my aim that it helps all those Carolines who don't make the headlines - of which there are many.

Kindness is important, as we never know what is happening in someone else's life. It is especially needed online. People power is strong and it can make a huge change in the world and this is what I envisage happening with Social Media Kindness Day - it's already happening and I am seeing a small shift.

We are the first generation to use social media in the way that we do now, and we've got another generation coming up online looking at us as an example. We really need them to see kindness online. And that was the premise of Social Media Kindness Day.

WHAT HAS CLUBHOUSE DONE FOR YOU OR OTHERS?
Clubhouse has given me a voice in a way that I couldn't find on any other social media platform. But it has made me be active on other platforms too. It's made it possible for me to share the cause I want to talk about, and it's been amazing to see how other people have connected to that message. I've loved sharing my message where there is live feedback. I have met some amazing people who I can pick up the phone to if I need their help with anything. Those I have met on Clubhouse feel like family - a Clubhouse family. When I've been off the app for a number of days, I've had my Clubhouse family contact me to see if I am okay. Clubhouse has also made the world a much smaller place.

I use Clubhouse on my own terms, where I show up when I want to rather than when I feel I have to. But I like the low maintenance of it too. By that I mean it's not standing in front of a camera, with my hair and make-up done, making sure the lighting is good and then doing the editing. All it requires is me picking up the phone and speaking. It's just me, my voice and my message, which is true authenticity.

Being an early adopter of the app, I have been pleased to see that there is no trolling - or not any I've seen. I also like how the founders of Clubhouse have said there's zero tolerance on trolling. Naturally, there will be disruption of stages the more people that are on it. But I hope this is called out quickly and made clear it is not accepted on this app. I think there will be things other social media companies can learn from Clubhouse.

For the clients I look after, there are some who want their social media managed by others. This has been possible with Facebook, Twitter and Instagram and the followers are not always aware that it is not the celebrity posting themselves. With Clubhouse, you have to show up as yourself. You can't outsource this. It HAS to be you, which is great and gives access to said celebrity like no other platform.

You can also choose how deep you want the connections to go, by taking it offline and I have with phone calls, WhatsApp and Zoom calls. This has varied from personal connections of friendships to business connections. It's that type of connection that I've been wanting and haven't got from any other platform.

WHAT DOES YOUR FUTURE LOOK LIKE BECAUSE OF CLUBHOUSE?
People sharing their stories is how we connect as humans. And that's what Clubhouse is - people sharing stories in an authentic way. It's been amazing to see. For the future, it has opened up a world of opportunity for me. From having business contacts all over the world, to joint venture opportunities - I'm already seeing some of that come to fruition.

Social Media Kindness Day is a recent initiative, so Clubhouse has definitely amplified that message by spreading it worldwide from the comfort of my home. It's also got others passionate about getting on board with that message and taking it even further. It is my heart's work and it is wonderful seeing how it's being spread. Due to Clubhouse, I even have a podcast about kindness coming out very soon.

CLUBHOUSE TOP TIPS

1. It's simple. Just get involved. Raise your hand, get on stage and share your message. We all have a message to share and you won't know how powerful or impactful your message can be if you're just sitting in the audience. Sitting in the audience and learning is amazing too, but let people hear your voice – your true authentic you. You may even surprise you.

2. We are all capable of making an impact in this world. When you have a worldwide audience available at your fingertips, that can hear your voice, then why wouldn't you use it to the best of your ability to share the impact you want to make?

3. Take any connections you make on Clubhouse offline because that's where the real magic happens. Everyone is wanting the same thing.

4. The only thing I would say to be careful of is advice. There's a lot of advice being given out, so I would just say be careful with how you use that advice. It's not always right. And if you're giving out feedback to anyone, always ask if it's okay to give your feedback. It's much more constructive giving feedback/advice when someone is open to it and has welcomed it.

5. Don't judge Clubhouse as just another social media app. I would say to get on it, see what it's about and just have fun with it.

Gillian Harding
@gills

🌹 Founder of Stem – NYC, LA, The Hamptons | 👗 Created the Gasparee by Gillian Harding fashion brand | 🛫 Built a hospitality startup | 📱 Founded Tech Startup 'Checkkin' coming 2022 | 🏛 Building a new way to send money abroad to help those in need

WHY ARE YOU ON CLUBHOUSE?

A VC who has invested in Clubhouse, called me and said, 'Gillian, I want you to come on board, it's the perfect platform for you and who you are in the world. You can empower so many people - come and check it out.' He sent me an invite, and then about five other people sent me invitations that day. So I just joined up!

WHAT IS YOUR STORY?

I'm originally from Trinidad and Tobago and now live in New York City. When I was living in the countryside of Trinidad and Tobago, I had big dreams for my life. Every Saturday morning I would watch our black and white television, while a stylish woman, Elsa Klensch, interviewed famous artists and interior decorators who lived overseas. I told my grandparents that my dream was to move to America and become someone successful, so I can make a difference back in my country and I know I can. My dream was to be a fashion designer, interior decorator, to have my own business and to have someone write about me in a magazine! Although my dream was strong, I felt I had no way of coming to

America because it was so very expensive to get a visa and you had to have a lot of money in the bank, which we didn't have.

But then, my life changed. A good friend of mine was studying at Georgetown University and he would come home every summer to visit. One summer he told us his friend's brother was coming to Trinidad to be the American ambassador. I got invited to the welcoming party and met him, a white guy from Iowa, and then we started to talk to each other every single day.

And then we ended up dating. He said he wanted to change the nature of our friendship. He said, 'I'm crazy about you.' So we started to date, and although I was happy, I had no interest in becoming an ambassador's wife because I was still passionate about the dream I had for my life. He gave me a multiple indefinite visa to come to America, and then everything I dreamt about my life actually happened. I became a fashion designer, interior decorator and an entrepreneur. They even wrote about me in a magazine. Everything I saw in my future from my life in Trinidad happened, even bigger than I even imagined.

WHAT HAS CLUBHOUSE DONE FOR YOU OR OTHERS?
Clubhouse was a life-changing moment for me. I know a lot of people got depressed during COVID-19, I myself got COVID-19 which was a life-changing moment for me, but I didn't get depressed and continued to live my life.

With every breakdown there can be a breakthrough, and I thought about who I wanted to be coming out of COVID-19, and that was a woman of great empathy and compassion, empowering other people to see a positive future. I knew we could all use this time during lockdown to come out with an amazing future. So that's what I did. Clubhouse is a platform where I was able to help a lot of people who were launching their startups who got stuck. I spent a lot of time empowering my friends to be greater than themselves, to live a life of gratitude; so that after COVID-19 they could be doing well and thriving.

Clubhouse gave me the ability to empower other people to see a different future than what they're living in at the moment. Some people had no future. People were just existing and trying to find their way. You know, they were stuck in the past. I had the opportunity to come share my story and to say, 'Hey, if I can come from the bushes of Trinidad and Tobago with some big dreams, everyone can choose a bigger life.' It makes no sense to me for American citizens to choose to live a small life. Go and create a platform or startup with something where you can solve a problem in the world. It's been an amazing journey and allowed me to share my story, which in turn has empowered others.

When I first started on Clubhouse, I saw it as an incredible opportunity to do some 'good' in the world. I came across someone who was looking for a kidney, and I thought, 'Oh my God, this is amazing.' Clubhouse really can be a platform for doing good in the world.

I live a very authentic life, and it's very important to me to be doing good and supporting others in the world. So it was always my intention to use Clubhouse for the greater good.

WHAT DOES YOUR FUTURE LOOK LIKE BECAUSE OF CLUBHOUSE?
I've started a club called Women Supporting Women, which has given me the opportunity to empower women. That journey is about supporting women to have thriving lives and for them to see a future that is way bigger than themselves. So that is the future that I'm aiming for.

And for myself, I have a startup which is called QWIKK, and it's a platform for immigrants and refugees from Latin America and the Caribbean, as a way of moving money cheaper and faster, using blockchain technology. So I've been meeting a lot of people on Clubhouse who have been helping me with my startup fund, and I never in my wildest dream thought I would connect with these people. It has been transformational.

CLUBHOUSE TOP TIPS

1. Well, there's 13 million amazing people on Clubhouse, and many of them just go in and listen. My tip is to share - don't just sit back in the audience. Get up on the stage and share about what you're doing, what's happening to you, what breakdowns you have, especially if there's something that you can say that will add any sort of value.

2. Offer to help. Life is about give and take. I find the people who are very successful in Clubhouse are adding value to other people's lives and supporting other people, and in turn, people are supporting them.

3. Have a purpose or intention. There are amazing possibilities for transformation if you play the game and be part of the greater good.

4. There's a lot of amazing stuff going on - just try to be part of it. Don't sit back in the audience and think that life is going to happen 'to' you.

Neil Sheth
@neilsheth

🎨 Digital content & marketing strategist | 💼 Founder @ Bubbli Digital (SEO agency) & Writefully (content creation) | 🏃 Former Investment Banking Consultant | 🏢 Works with 5-figure and 8-figure companies | 🌱 Grown and scaled over 200 businesses using content marketing and SEO | ✏️ We write over 200,000 words every month

WHY ARE YOU ON CLUBHOUSE?

I came across Clubhouse in December 2020 when everyone was raving about it. I almost avoided it because I thought it was just another social media platform. I didn't really want to add it to my list of 'things to do.'

But there was just so much hype around it and I thought I had nothing to lose, so I went to the App Store but I couldn't get in, so I left it. But then, a few days later, a friend actually just let me in and the rest is history, as they say.

WHAT IS YOUR STORY?

I'm based in London and run a content marketing agency called Bubbly Digital.

In 2009, I launched my very first website while working in investment banking. I spent £20,000 on it, and launched after six or seven months but we couldn't even force our family or friends to buy through that website, let alone customers. I realised I needed to understand digital marketing. I was still working in investment banking by day, in companies like Goldman Sachs and Barclays Capital, and by night, I was obsessed with the idea of launching an online business.

So, that's what I did. I launched website after website; a public speaking site, a luxury gift store, a travel experiences site and so many others. Some of these actually worked and when I first started seeing sales, it was amazing. I loved the idea of not knowing who's buying. It was crazy. So I doubled down. I learnt content marketing, content creation, and tried to hire a few agencies and experts because I was still going into my banking job by day. I was really busy and suddenly realised I knew more than them. I didn't trust them and thought, 'Why don't I just try and do this for myself?'

So, I hired my own team, did my own marketing and then thought, you know what, 'Why don't I just do this for other businesses?' So, it was 2017 when I had the guts to take the leap. I decided to create a content marketing agency. We started in the first year working from home in my home office. It was me doing everything, including sales and marketing. Over time, we grew real partnerships and built the team. So, yeah, that's kind of how I fell into it.

WHAT HAS CLUBHOUSE DONE FOR YOU OR OTHERS?

A large portion of our business is built up by referrals and partnerships. It's website design companies referring to us and integrating us into their workflow, as well as paid ad agencies integrating us. We've got a handful of really good partners who we trust, and who trust us. We pass work to each other because we know they're going to do a great job.

Clubhouse has pretty much taken that concept to a whole new level. We're launching a new content creation brand, and I've already got a bunch of people going, 'Oh my God, all of our people need this. Sign us up.' So, I've moved from the concept depending on two or three really good partners to potentially ten or fifteen in the space of three months.

And with those two or three partners, our relationships have been developed over four years, because they don't just start off by sending you loads of work, they give you one piece of work, wait to hear feedback and then they see how you work with them. Over time, they trust you. And it's the same with us. We don't just send our clients to our partners, we make sure they're going to deliver on what they say. But Clubhouse has literally opened up the doors to friends and businesses who already trust each other because we spend all day on Clubhouse speaking to the same people over and over again.

You start to quickly understand who's an awesome person, who's going to take care of your customers and who isn't. So we've pretty much increased our trusted partners to about fifteen businesses in two or three months.

WHAT DOES YOUR FUTURE LOOK LIKE BECAUSE OF CLUBHOUSE?
I'm beginning to be more strategic on Clubhouse than I was for the initial three months.

It's a bit like a sprint race. You know, how do I build a Clubhouse following as quickly as possible? I've pretty much stopped publishing and posting on all other social media channels, because the reach on Clubhouse is incredible. However, I don't think it's sustainable for one's mind, or just from an overall marketing strategy perspective. It's time consuming and highly consuming in terms of mental energy.

So, I'll be more strategic along the lines of still creating great rooms, but maybe doing less of them, sharing out the workload, collaborating, and considering my strategy as Android opens up, bringing in customers or people that want to work with us by integrating audiences that exist elsewhere. I don't think doing that at the moment would make sense, but in the future it makes total sense to do it two ways.

CLUBHOUSE TOP TIPS

1. Build your relationships and connections. It is not all about doing 'me me me.' Go to other rooms, and other people's stages you don't know and just ask them really good questions that you are actually interested in finding out about, because listeners can tell if you're interested or not. If someone asks good questions, I want them on my stage.

2. Forge alliances with like-minded people. It's good for everyone; good for the audience and good for you, and generally good for your experience. It's a great opportunity to collaborate with others. Even if there's only ten people in a room, if everyone's interested and engaged, it's just like going to the pub or going for a walk.

3. Slide into WhatsApp. Okay, so you've heard the phrase, 'Slide into DMs' – DM on Instagram is a good way to connect with people and start to build a relationship. But once you've got that relationship, you don't really want to be another message in 100 messages. You want to be that one message, a connection to a friend, so that's why I suggest WhatsApp. The people in my WhatsApp are people I'm going to keep in contact with regardless of where Clubhouse or other social media goes.

126

4. Strategically plan your rooms. Pick a really good topic, something that is going to get people to click. I wouldn't suggest going to clickbait, but there is an element of grabbing attention with the topic of your room. Be strategic about the time of day that works for your audience, and for the people who will join your room. Get some awesome energetic people on the panel that can bring value. Choose people with not just the same expertise, same experience, or the same culture. Mix it up. Get different cultures into the conversation, because you will start to appeal to more people and help them feel more comfortable.

5. Bring your energy. I've been in rooms where conversations are mundane; they're boring. You can hear it in the person's voice. They're bored. They're bored on stage. People aren't going to stick around, they're going to bounce off the engagement ring. The stickiness is going to be fairly low. You want to be just below Tony Robbins' level of energy! Learn how he does it, how he jumps up before he goes on stage, just get in that mindset, get active, bring the energy, because people will hear it in the conversation. And yes, it's tiring, but you want people to leave that room saying, 'You know what? I really want to join him next time because he livens up my day.' So bring your energy.

Pam Sotiropoulou Frigo
@pamsotir

💵 Investor | 🏃 Forging Athletic Mindset | ⭐ Passion for Nature, Food, Art & Design | 💼 MBA in Finance | 📈 25 years experience with foreign exchange trading

WHY ARE YOU ON CLUBHOUSE?

In early 2021, an exercise coach told me about this new app called Clubhouse and as soon as I got into it, I just fell in love with it.

I love that the design is so fluid and open. I can go into a room and just listen or I can participate and be a part of the conversation. Clubhouse is deceptively simple, yet ultimately powerful and it revolves around the authenticity of the voice.

It is a total immersion experience, and what I mean by that is, you come in and you not only learn, but you hold many hats at the same time. And in doing so, you're learning in your interaction. It just becomes that much more meaningful. So with Clubhouse, you learn, you inspire, and you get inspired. You share, you help, you collaborate and connect. In addition, you can connect off-app with those who resonate with you and go even deeper.

I love the value I gain just by listening to people speak and I'm continually amazed by the wonderfully interesting people I am coming across through Clubhouse – people I'd never have encountered in any other way.

WHAT IS YOUR STORY?

I am a real estate developer and an investor, based in London. My whole professional career has been around pattern recognition and investing in areas of untapped potential.

During my investment banking days, spanning over twenty years, I bought and sold currencies from around the world. In the financial world, I've been very blessed to be in the top tier of financial institutions during incredible innovation and disruption.

I have a passion for nature, food, wine and design. Right now I'm working on my vision of building a real estate hospitality development with a boutique hotel in Greece; one which broadens the way hospitality currently works. The hospitality industry is very transactional right now. It's all about filling the rooms and providing service from arrival to departure. So the focus of the connection with the client is from the point of a physical stay. Yet, when a person books a holiday or an escape, evidence shows that their state changes from the time they enter the relationship – not just when they get to their destination. So, I want to tap into that; where the relationship, experience and community starts from the moment one contemplates a visit, using the virtual world to allow them to discover and connect with others before they arrive, and after they leave. Where the person can maintain the connections they have made and continue to have lasting connectivity with a vibrant community.

The real estate itself will be functional and adapted to the environment. The way it is constructed, the way it looks and the way customers are served, will all be in harmony with nature. Food will be locally sourced and fresh, as the location is abundant and full of life. There is nature all around, with protected sand dunes, the sea and the countryside. It will be a perfect place for people to meander and discover themselves.

With the growing interest in self-development and discovery, I'm creating the perfect destination for masterminds, coaching groups and communities who want to work on themselves in simplicity and flow.

In a sense, what I am creating with my hospitality brand and the vibrant virtual community is the same kind of fluidity that is around the rooms in Clubhouse.

WHAT HAS CLUBHOUSE DONE FOR YOU OR OTHERS?
By participating in Clubhouse, I have the opportunity of using my authentic voice to build communities and assets. I help others internalise the incredible power of turning longevity and impact into assets instead of liabilities. For instance, in Clubhouse, I hold a daily room where we discuss issues around kisnature.com; a community-led initiative that inspires people around their impact, and gets them excited about the integration of the Sustainable Development Goals (17 SDGs) with internalising nature's wisdom. In doing so, I've been able to connect with ordinary people doing extraordinary things.

WHAT DOES YOUR FUTURE LOOK LIKE BECAUSE OF CLUBHOUSE?
Clubhouse is an integral part of my day. I do have an intention … and that is I believe we all have a duty to reconnect with nature, no matter what business we are in or which businesses we sup-

port. We need to be mindful of what that means in totality and in a holistic manner.

The future is to continue to use Clubhouse as a powerful tool to build vibrant communities around longevity, impact and being in harmony with nature. That is, to collaborate and connect, absorbing as much information as possible, and creating impact by doing and being the change.

If you look at the Internet revolution, that gave us information freely available to everyone. Then the mobile revolution gave us mobility and the ability to carry a computer and walk around with it. This third revolution is the digital revolution, and connectivity and community building are key drivers. That is what Clubhouse is all about.

A final thought is what is written on the Oracle at Delphi – 'Know Thyself.' That's what Clubhouse allows people to do by their participation.

CLUBHOUSE TOP TIPS

1. If you are new to Clubhouse, enter into it with a curious mind – explore, try different rooms, listen and learn. Take the opportunity to absorb what is happening in different rooms to see which ones give you value.

2. Participation is wonderful – coming on the stage and sharing – but it doesn't need to happen right away. Start as an observer and grow from there.

3. Consistency is really important – to build connections you need to show up regularly. At the same time, it is easy to get overwhelmed and caught up in the 24/7 nature of the platform, so strike a balance by finding the rooms and people who resonate with you. Most importantly, have fun and enjoy the process.

James Burtt
@jamesburtt

Brand Performance Expert | Audio Strategist | 🎧 Podcast Launch Expert | 🎙️ Managing Director 'Ultimate Podcast Group' | 🔊 Head of Creative 'Phonic Media' | 🎤 Podcaster 'Building The Brand' | 📺 Media Coach | ⭐ International Speaker | ➕ IPQA Accredited Peak Performance coach ➕ Accredited Master NLP Practitioner

WHY ARE YOU ON CLUBHOUSE?

I came across Clubhouse because one of my podcasting clients happens to be Natasha Hamilton from Atomic Kitten. She kept talking to me about this app and she's like, 'You've got to check it out. You really got to check out this audio social media app – it's right up your alley!' And I was like, 'Ah, nah - I'm not interested. I don't need another social media platform,' but she said she would send an invite anyway. So, she sent me an invite and I jumped in. I thought it was nonsense. I even did a podcast episode saying why Clubhouse is the biggest waste of time in 2021 (maybe)! I'm glad I gave myself that wiggle room because it wasn't long before I was hooked.

WHAT IS YOUR STORY?

I'm often referred to as The Podcast King. I've been in the branding, broadcast, entrepreneurial and radio space for fifteen years. I've been involved in the world of broadcast PR since 2006, when I worked for an agency just outside London. I didn't know what broadcast PR was but it sounded like a cool thing to be involved in. I needed a proper job because I'd been a cabaret singer up until that point and I needed something sensible because the music industry is a dodgy game. But it turned out that job was more focused on selling than it was about PR realistically.

So, I got really good at selling quite quickly, and I ended up, because I was good at selling, working with IBM, Thomas Cook, Nissan, Xbox, you know, those sorts of companies within the first eighteen months of being involved in the sector. I had a real fast ascent to becoming a branding and broadcast expert very quickly because I needed to be. You know the old analogy of 'if you're the dumbest person in the room, you're in the right room,' well, I was always the dumbest person in every single room I was in.

When I was learning that skill set of broadcasting, I fell in love with the idea of being a radio presenter, I'd always loved radio anyway. So, I wanted to get on the other side of the microphone. I got a job on a national digital radio station called Amazing Radio; a station that plays no adverts and nothing but new and unsigned music.

They brought in the ex-head of Radio One who was going to make some sweeping changes. I nudged my mate and said, 'Hey, sweeping changes - we're in the right place.' Unfortunately, his first sweeping change was to sack me and my mate, because he thought we were rubbish. He probably had a point to be fair. So I went and worked in sponsorship and promotion for a big radio group. Then I did some property investment stuff, before coming back full circle.

I launched our first podcast in 2017, having sat on the idea for five years. And I was thinking, 'You know what, podcast is a bit like a broadcast and a bit like radio - but no-one can sack you from your own show. That's the ideal place for me.' And it was. So, the day I launched my first show, Tim Ferriss was number one, Gary Vee was number three, and I was the meat of the influencer sandwich, sat at number two. So that worked out quite well. And fast forward to now, as of last week, I've launched 136 top-rated podcasts for clients around the world. So that's my broadcast background - that's me in a nutshell.

WHAT HAS CLUBHOUSE DONE FOR YOU OR OTHERS?

Clubhouse has opened up a whole world of opportunities that I didn't really know were there. It's given me the ability to have the sort of impact that large influencers have on other platforms, maybe I have an unfair advantage because of my broadcasting background. I was spending hours on Clubhouse, and I'm sure other contributors to the book have said this as well, but I asked myself, 'What's the purpose of this? What's my outcome here? What am I actually doing here?' As an accredited coach I am focused on outcome thinking.

Then I set myself a challenge. I said, 'If I don't make a thousand quid directly attributed through this platform, and not just trickle down revenue, but a thousand quid in the next ten days, then I'm getting off it.' Well, I made about five or six grand in that week. And then I could say, 'Okay, well that's an income-producing activity.'

I then had the, how shall I put it, 'Come to Jesus' conversation with my wife. Clubhouse is an income-producing activity, a place where I can get leads for our business and that's why I would be spending so much time on it. So, that's what I did. You know the analogy of 'you are exactly where you're supposed to be right now,' well, it's never been more apt for me than right now. The fifteen years of broadcast PR branding, getting businesses right, getting some businesses wrong, and going down the coaching route, to create a very successful business with a couple of business partners for a few years. It made a lot of money, but it was not always good for my soul or my moral compass. Yet, all of those things I've done have led me to this place now, where actually the audio space has never been more important or prevalent. I've got the background and the expertise from both sides of the microphone to maximise the opportunity.

It also feeds back more broadly than that, it feeds back into the thing that makes me most happy, which is making other people happy. I just love having a laugh, I love having fun, and this gives me the opportunity to be an influencer in a congruent way, where the bigger your influence, the more happiness and fun you can bring to people. This is the ultimate platform for the class clown, I'd say.

WHAT DOES YOUR FUTURE LOOK LIKE BECAUSE OF CLUBHOUSE?
The future for me on Clubhouse is going to depend on what happens next with the platform. One of the key things to understand, especially with a new platform, is you have to be agile and you have to be flexible. What's working today, won't necessarily work tomorrow. You have to be willing to change with the times. Very carefully look at what's happening on the platform and what the data is telling you.

There are some great data platforms out there now. You have to read the data and be able to understand what that data is telling you. For example, the things we look at closely in our rooms that we run, is 'listen time.' We're not so interested in the numbers of people in the room or who comes through the room, or the peak number of people who are in the room at any given time. The biggest metric for us, if we're getting it right or wrong, is listen time.

We've had weeks recently where our average listen time is twenty-plus minutes – amazing! The average listen time on Clubhouse is about nine minutes and the average listen time for generalised broadcast is seven-point-two minutes. Yes, I'm a data geek. And the thing to really understand is what your outcome is. So, we're building an audio social media based agency in the back end. For us, it's about understanding what the sector is doing more broadly. It's not just about Clubhouse; there's other offshoots. You've got Twitter spaces, Reddit talk, and Discord, so I think it's about looking more broadly at audio as a platform, rather than being too focused on something singularly, like Clubhouse. There are other platforms that are going to take a chunk out of their marketplace, so we need to be willing and agile enough to move with the times. And when Facebook, YouTube or whoever buys them, by the way, I'm going to put a prediction out here - I think it could be Spotify - when Spotify buys this platform, you're then playing the game according to their rules. And fundamentally, if you base your existence on someone else's platform, you're always playing by somebody else's rules if you don't own that platform. So, watch what's happening in the marketplace and be willing to be agile and read the data the platform is giving you.

CLUBHOUSE TOP TIPS

1. Lead with value. I cannot say that enough. There's a lot of positive marketers out there, like Gary Vee who have made it popular and famous to lead with value, but a lot of people who say it, don't do it. What you put into Clubhouse you will get out, if you genuinely lead with value. It can be a massive time drain so understand what your outcome is for it. What do you want to be there for? Lead with value is the best thing I can suggest.

2. Get around some good people with the same mentality. The way we've been able to blow up what we've been doing on Clubhouse is as a collective, and having that collective mentality. Four or five of us got together and jumped into a WhatsApp group in January/February time just to support each other's rooms. That's all we were there to do, frankly, was to support each other, but that became a business. And it's become a brand; a friendship, a community, a culture, and an extended family, you know, thousands of people from all over the world, because we've all got the same mentality. Make sure your vision and your values are aligned with that community of people you put yourself around, because that's the fastest way to grow your community in the right direction.

3. Don't be a spammy salesman. There's nothing that turns people off quicker than spammy sales-people. I'm really strict and often get called rude if someone starts pitching and they're not one of our regular community members or family members, I just simply put them back in the audience.

4. If you're not the message you preach, then Clubhouse is not the platform for you. If you do not have genuine expertise in the subject that you're talking about, you will get found out, which is why I love this platform. There's been so many rooms I've been in and someone will jump up and talk about marketing or sales or whatever, and then you dig into it and they don't know their arse from their elbow, frankly, so only jump up to give advice on this platform if you're an expert practitioner of your craft.

Debo Harris FCA
@deboharris

❓ I ask great questions | 🎩 Non-Exec Dir of £mill orgs | Career in M&A, Finance | Founder & CEO ConfidenceVault.com | 👰 Deputy President of 🐥◎ Founder of the ConfidentWomen Club

WHY ARE YOU ON CLUBHOUSE?

Originally, it was for fun and the social aspect, but I've moved on to using it in a much more purposeful way.

It's been five weeks now on Clubhouse, and I am using it for three things: to access the global community; to build my tribe of unapologetically ambitious women through the three clubs I run (ConfidentWomen, The Business of Money and InspiringTomorrow); and to reconnect with people in the world of finance and venture capital as a non-executive director.

WHAT IS YOUR STORY?

I graduated with a Civil Engineering degree, but went on to train as an accountant, based in the City of London, with one of the largest professional services firms in the world. I currently work as a non-executive director in multimillion-pound organisations that deliver quality healthcare, education, property, and more recently, finance. I'm also the CEO of The Confidence Vault, a UK sponsor mentoring service offering women access to corporations willing to help women achieve their next-level greatness.

We help them to build their brand and connect them to senior leaders in their dream careers so they can walk through the door and sit confidently at the boardroom table, either as an executive, a non-executive director, or as CEO of their own business.

When I was in school, a teacher told me if I 'worked really hard, kept my nose clean and my head down that perhaps I could get a job in the local supermarket and rise to the dizzying heights of a shop floor supervisor'. There is nothing wrong with working in retail or customer service, but as I had plans to be a civil engineer, that future was not for me. I'd done the research, so it wasn't helpful to be told how high my ambition should be.

And I learnt very early on that there is just one word you can use to disarm microaggressors and unconscious bias. And you don't have to be the most educated of people to use it. When the sixth form tutor told my grandmother I should 'do secretarial work and become a good secretary,' my grandmother said, 'Nevertheless.' And that's all she said; it wasn't a whole sentence. She just said that one word. And in effect, it was, 'Yeah, I hear you, but I don't accept it.' In order to address challenges, you sometimes have to put your head up and your face into the wind and say, 'nevertheless.'

So, I read Civil Engineering with an internship on the East Coast in the United States. I enjoyed learning how massive buildings and major structures go up, and stay up, but realised, unfortunately, that I really didn't like working outside. A bit of a problem as the majority of my life as a civil engineer in the UK would be in cold, rainy weather. I didn't want to do that. At all.

I'd also become interested in understanding how businesses went up and stayed up and heard about audit. I looked into it and thought, 'Yeah, that would be a great way to see how a business performs.' You get to nose around and find out how businesses work, how their finances failed and speak to the management. So, I decided I would go into Banking & Financial Services audit.

I loved working in financial services audit. I also found I got pleasure from working closely with people who were starting up businesses, particularly social businesses or businesses that democratised the workplace. And that's why I moved into venture capital and angel investing, and ultimately the move into non-executive directorships.

I think I started my board roles probably a decade earlier than most people, while I was still in full-time work, because I realised that you can't change cultures, organisations or the quality of service from the outside. I've been able to use my finance skills as an auditor, but also my governance skills and my strong focus on risk management and equality. I've really enjoyed trying to address the unconscious bias that people have about members of the community they may not otherwise meet.

My volunteering is very much on holding the door open for diversity, because I knew what it was like for me finding my feet. Financial services is still a male-dominated industry and women are often not paid the same as their male peers. On top of that, when you look across or upwards in your organisation and don't see anyone who's like you, whether in terms of gender or race, you start to reconsider if the people in that industry are people you want to work with.

I believe that greater cognitive diversity in teams across an organisation allows you to harness greater innovation - and that's needed more than ever. You get the wisdom of the crowd; a crowd of diverse views focused on the central point of delivering quality care, whether it's in education, health, financial services, or the arts.

My volunteering around women equality is very much along the same lines. Women have to work twice as hard, and provide twice as much evidence at recruitment, in work meetings and often in their evaluations. They're often interrupted and spoken over by men in meetings, up to three times more than their male peers. And as all research shows, these stats are worse for women of colour. As a woman of colour on boards, I am encouraged when impactful allies show up for women in general, and women of colour in particular, in areas where they are not well represented. Women need more great women in the boardroom to get the 'tipping point' in behaviour; more allies who push back against the microaggression, allies who can champion, who can act as advocates, who can hold the space, who can amplify our voices.

One of the things that I'm planning to do is hold space so people have the opportunity for us to move away from just rhetoric and actually start to embed anti-racism into 'business as usual.' Another benefit from this is a greater chance to harness cognitive diversity and as a result, greater innovation.

WHAT HAS CLUBHOUSE DONE FOR YOU OR OTHERS?

I really enjoy talking to people. Clubhouse converted me from a rather jaded view of using audio technology for just meetings and work. It's connected me to some fantastic people, some of them maybe half an hour away from where I live, some halfway around the world. It's allowed me to understand what my purpose is in terms of the value I give and the ethics I stand for. In the early days it controlled my life and my sleep patterns! It can sometimes be all-consuming; whether it's me sitting in the audience, rolling my eyes in annoyance at some comment in the audience, which then makes me put my hand up and give another point of view.

Clubhouse has allowed me to celebrate the diversity we have in this world and the fact that in the right rooms you are not judged on your gender or skin colour, but by the content of your conversation. This democratises the voice within Clubhouse. And I mean, honestly, if you're in a room where author, multimillion-pound bestseller and motivational speaker, Hal Elrod, is talking about *The Miracle Morning,* then answering questions from the audience and then giving a mini coaching session, that's pretty amazing. You can show up for Harvard Business School classes, or ConfidentWomen Wednesday where women practice their skills of self-promotion and support. Then you can jump into another room with Tiffany Haddish, and then another room where you can listen to Elon Musk or Mark Zuckerberg. That's pretty amazing.

Even better, you can join a cosy room chat about the technical issues to colonise Mars, who would be in the first wave, and whether inequality will be perpetuated in the same way. Or whether they will ship prisoners from the overpopulated prisons in, say the USA, onto spaceships to be the first pioneers, as in recent history, who cut the path and dig the foundations alongside the robotics on the surface of Mars. And that was just a Tuesday. You don't find that anywhere else; you'd be exhausted if you had to travel to join all of these chats. But that's what Clubhouse does, it brings people together and it's been a great experience for me. Even though sometimes I have missed hours of sleep, I have not lost sleep over the amount of hours that I have spent on Clubhouse.

I've seen in Clubhouse the conversations around mental health and combating isolation. The platform gives people opportunities to talk about these sorts of things. Overall, I think the benefit of Clubhouse is that you can now start talking and coordinating global involvement of some of the most intractable problems people have seen in the world, whether it's climate change, gender equality or any of the other strategic UN sustainable development goals. That is the greatest opportunity for members of Clubhouse.

It has had a big impact on people's ability to come together and talk about issues that previously were not part of 'polite' dinner conversation. And I don't think that's a bad thing.

WHAT DOES YOUR FUTURE LOOK LIKE BECAUSE OF CLUBHOUSE?
I don't think it's going to change. I very quickly gained my focus for being on Clubhouse and I've stuck with it. The future, for me, is very much more of the same. And it's growing. I do think the exponential trajectory of followers people got if they joined in the summer of 2020 was already slowing by the time I joined.

Some people are quite aggressive in the way they go about putting themselves on stage to demand you follow them. I'm not a believer in that. Give great quality in every room you join and followers will be drawn to you. So, in five weeks, I'd already topped 3000 followers. Clubhouse definitely pays you for the time that you invest in it.

If you give value, if you go to rooms with an open mind and a genuine desire to add value, and to listen with empathy and to challenge with respect, and stick with your values, it will pay you back in terms of people who want to spend more time with you, people who follow you, and in terms of what you get in your hallway. That's what I mean by the payback.

It is a symbiotic relationship. Clubhouse provides something that the pandemic and our lockdowns had taken from a lot of people. I didn't mind if I was out and about or working from home, so Clubhouse actually expanded my network. I can see more of that. It may slow down because of the sheer volume of people that are coming onto the platform, and the Android users now joining, but overall, I think there's a richness in the people. And a space, room or stage for everyone.

With Clubhouse, you make of it what you will. There are some people who have garbage in their hallway, but that's because they've spent time focusing on what I call the 'ratchet rooms' - rooms set up to trigger, antagonise and belittle one group of people. However, as the Clubhouse platform is quite forgiving, you can change what you see over time by changing the people you follow. The founders are also keen to find and upgrade the beta version with new functions that enhance user experience. But it is up to you to choose where you focus your time.

I like to use the mnemonic SIZES:

S – Size. Room size is important. Pick your rooms, pick the room size that works for you. Remember though that there is some value in all of them.

I - Intention. Come to Clubhouse with an intention. If you come and just mosey around, you may miss out on something. Be intentional in your searches, and the rooms you go in to. Be intentional with the people you follow, because who you follow will determine the quality of your experience. It's also okay for your intention to change from time to time.

Z – Zero. Zero care over how you look. Your profile picture is down to you. How you look has zero to do with who you interact with. It's more about how you show up. Remember, your bio is also important. Consider the quality of your conversations and people will connect with you. Outside of Clubhouse, have an Instagram or Twitter account so people can contact you, that's the fastest way people contact each other. With other challenger apps coming onstream it's been interesting to find people meeting in Spaces (on Twitter), or using nēdl or Racket apps talking about ... Clubhouse!

E - Engage. Engage with people, engage with heart and always try to empower the people you're talking with. There are some pretty vulnerable people on Clubhouse. There are some people who are scared and hurt and you have no idea what your words will do. So, always try to engage, uplift, empower, embrace and do it with empathy.

S - Stick with it. You're never going to get 46 million followers or connections if you don't stick with Clubhouse.

When I started Clubhouse, there were approx. one million users, now there are 10 million+ users every single day and new Android users create an exponential growth in user numbers. That's growth week after week. I see Clubhouse removes the physical distance between citizens of all the countries of the world. Our borders are man-made, created through conquest and not consensus, and I love being able to access people across the globe through Clubhouse, and the valuable conversations we have. Join us, we're friendly!

Ashley Shipman
@ashleyshipman

💰 Sales & Marketing growth expert | 🗣 International speaker | 📧 Focused on amplifying you or your business message| 🦸 Proud Husband and Father of 2 | 📈 Creates high performing individuals and teams to become elite level performers | 👁 Expert Judge "The Big Idea Challenge" | 🎧 Podcaster "The Winners Club"

WHY ARE YOU ON CLUBHOUSE?

I was in a sales mastermind which I head up with a partner, and I saw that a 'big gun' influencer, possibly Les Brown, was about to 'go live on Clubhouse.' As I'm into marketing and sales, any new social media catches my interest, and I was like, 'Tell me what this is … I need to know!'

I teach and help clients with their sales and marketing, so part of my job is social media and to know what's going on in that space. Someone in the mastermind mentioned they'd been on Clubhouse for two days, and I had to be part of it; I insisted they send me the link!

WHAT IS YOUR STORY?

I started in a company in financial services and within a couple of years, I was running the team. I worked my way through the corporate ladder, but I wasn't happy. I was in a bad state of mind, so instead I started helping out and training the new guys in the industry, building the team and tracking the results, to check that I knew what I was talking about and I didn't just get lucky. The hard work really did pay off with the knowledge and expertise I gained.

During that journey, I probably started and failed around six different businesses through doing things out of stupidity, thinking I needed multiple streams of income before I made one solidly work, and spreading myself too thin. Name an industry and I'll tell you how I've been part of it and what not to do. It was pretty embarrassing. But you live and learn – me thinking I was an entrepreneur because of everything going on, but nothing was working properly.

I had to have the realisation to step back. If you think about a diamond; it comes out of the earth brown, and needs to have all its edges cut to become worth something.

At the time, I was being headhunted from every angle. 'Can you come help my sales team?' Offering me X, Y and Z big salaries, and big bonuses. When I spoke to people around me, they said if I was that in demand, I could turn my experience into a business. And from there, the rest is history; lots of ups and downs, lots of dry months, lots of good months, and now it's going really well.

One thing I didn't know, and I'm going to be honest, I used to suffer with depression and anxiety, but I didn't really know it. I would bounce of the walls and not know what was going on, but it was all down to me not being satisfied. If there's no self-achievement when you walk away at the end of the day, it can have a massive effect on anyone's mental health.

So I was asked, 'What do you love to do?' And I said, 'I love to see people go from A to B – to see their achievements.' And finally I was part of that journey. I don't give to receive, but I do believe life and business depends on the energy you put out there. And it has worked in my favour. I don't ask, I just give.

Some people say you can't fill your glass from an empty cup, but I'll recharge my cup in other ways. Me seeing you progress is filling my cup. I've always said, 'Give me an inch, and I'll give you a mile.'

WHAT HAS CLUBHOUSE DONE FOR YOU OR OTHERS?

I'd been in Clubhouse for about a week, when all I wanted to do was jump up on stage, network and talk to people. But I'd been joining rooms with people I follow and respect – those whose books I'd read, videos I'd watched or training I'd done - and I was in awe; like their number one fan sitting in the audience. When it came to asking questions, I was forever clicking that 'hand raise' button, but no-one would let me speak. It was like 'who are you?' And even when I did get to speak, I got stage fright and fumbled my words; I just couldn't get my words out because suddenly I was in a position where I might be able to talk to people I never thought I would have access to.

I hung in there for a couple of days, and I still couldn't get to speak. I felt I had to keep trying. I had to smash through walls to talk to these people as the opportunity was there. I may as well just read their book or watch their video. But then, all of sudden, I realised that there were eighty-five people with their hands raised, all wanting to communicate and connect. There was a big gap between the people on stage, and the people in the audience. So, I started reaching out and connecting to the people in the audience via their Instagram, and creating relationships with them. I also was connecting with the people on stage asking their advice – with no response of course. And I thought, if there isn't a space for us in the audience, I'll create one, and if it doesn't work I'll take the fall. 'Screw it, I'm doing it!'

So I started a room, because I wanted to give a space for everyone to have a voice, and the first one I did, I was shaking, but as soon as someone came in the room, I would bring them up on stage as I knew they wanted to do that. It was a safe space where people could get up and speak.

The first room I had was four people – including three of my friends! The second day was three friends, two people from the mastermind and two random people. Soon there were fifteen people in the room. It wasn't long, I think a week went by, and the big influencers started dropping into my room, but they didn't automatically get centre stage. It's a creative space for people who want to have their voices heard and to connect with others to help grow their businesses. As the audience started building, the numbers were up and down, but people were connecting.

I don't sell in my rooms – that's not how I work. I have got products and things to sell, but my intention in business is to connect and build collaborations. I would rather build a relationship with someone who may be able to open doors for me down the line with the right intention. I'm not in it to smash the audience to buy quick or sell people short, I'm here for the long-term. I did trial the sales pitching style for a few days, but it didn't sit right with me.

The thing with Clubhouse at the start, was that no-one knew the rules. I was like a rabbit in headlights. I had to come back to reality, and ask myself my vision and purpose for this platform. If you do something consistently and authentically over and over again, the money is just a by-product of the service you offer.

Being on Clubhouse actually gave me a space to tell people what I do. It can be hard, in any space, to let others know what you do. When I was nineteen and twenty-one, I spent time trying to improve my personal brand, and to be honest, I had a lot of people making fun of me. It did knock my confidence. I had to take a step back, but I do have a lot of clients with a lot of clout. Being older now, I'm actively seeking to have my story out there, and I like to communicate and network. I'm no longer a nineteen-year-old trying to tell a fifty-year-old how to run their business – I know – what was I thinking right?! But hey, you live and you learn.

I'm out there now actively seeking, and I have space in my diary for networking – I need to be networking and working on relationships. Clubhouse has made that very easy. With lockdown in the UK, face to face networking has been impossible, so Clubhouse is the closest thing you can get to a networking event. However, Clubhouse is networking on steroids, and it's fast paced.

I've been named the King of Clubhouse. I didn't name myself that and I still don't put in my bio! I'm not one of those guys who says, 'Look at me, look at me,' but I get called it everywhere. I've now connected with people who I've followed for my whole entrepreneurial journey, and that has been priceless.

I've interviewed billionaires, multimillionaires, serious influencers, people of power, and hosted rooms for the government. One of the highlights was hosting scale up week in the winner's club. We hosted rooms for some big business influencers; they came to the club that we own to do that, so it's crazy. I've become really good friends with TV personalities, influencers, icons and professional footballers.

It's been amazing to give everyday people the opportunity to speak to famous and influential people. Even when I'm interviewing, I'm in awe, and yet so many of these guys are asking, 'What can I do for you, Ash? What are you looking for?' I always reply, 'Well, a relationship really,' and often that's the first time anyone has said that to them.

The thing is, with everyone I connect with these days, I'm true to my heart. That's not always been the case. I used to wear a three-piece suit and think I was someone I wasn't. And that attracted a lot of the wrong people.

I've realised that just being who I am is attracting a bigger network for me and really good conversations. It's that simple.

WHAT DOES YOUR FUTURE LOOK LIKE BECAUSE OF CLUBHOUSE?
I've had a lot of opportunities sent my way, which are all being worked on in the background. It's all due to the exposure. I am willing to put myself in a spot where I can be ridiculed or I can be loved and I'm only getting a little bit of ridicule at the moment, but I am being noticed by the right people.

With Clubhouse, I just want to make sure I offer a safe space and bring people into rooms that have a community and give them access to have their voice heard. I want a platform that incorporates training, education, coaching, masterclasses and solid, sound people from which to learn.

I'm not just about connecting with billionaires, I want people with knowledge and experience. Being financially sound is secondary to me. I know some phenomenal people who don't have serious bank balances. And I want those people around me because if I can provide a space where someone can go and connect the dots moving forward, I've done my job. I've done what I've set out to do.

So the future for me and Clubhouse is to keep doing what I'm doing, trying to diversify the room as much as possible, bring some new stuff, and bring some new ideas. It's not just my room, it's everyone's room; it's a community. My future is to keep the diversity up and keep it pumping and alive.

If I had access to a platform like this five or ten years ago, I'd be a lot further along my journey than I am now.

CLUBHOUSE TOP TIPS

1. Go with intention - I don't mean go and sell, sell, sell your product, but have a clear intention of why you want to use the app. Utilise the app as you see fit, and utilise your time while being there. It's the only social media where you can get real time interaction connections beyond any other app.

2. When you walk into a room, raise your hand. You aren't going to get a chance to get up and connect with people if your hand isn't raised.

3. While you're waiting for a question, or if you're on the stage or a co-host, make sure you reach out to the other co-hosts and take all relationships further than Clubhouse. It's very fast paced so it's always the next conversation that will be remembered. If you're in the audience, reach out and connect with anyone on the panel or in the audience because you've got like-minded people there.

4. Follow the rules of anyone's room. Respect the room and the club you are in.

5. Serve others - I love helping people, but it's come to light there are people who say it and people who do it. If you serve well enough you won't need to pitch your product or service. Build your credibility first – don't make it a pitchfest; make it educational, motivational and inspirational.

Danny Levin
@themosaic

◎ Walked away from a billion-dollar business opportunity | 🏃 Hitchhiked around the world to find happiness and inner peace | ⛏ Former Director of Business Development at Hay House | ✒ Author of The Mosaic | ◉ Visionary who listens | 📖 Storyteller | 🎙 Speaker | ⭐ Mentor | ➲ Guide

WHY ARE YOU ON CLUBHOUSE?

For me, who am I is a complicated question. I have lived a lot of lives this lifetime and so it is hard for me to give the breath of my life in a simple answer. I have had the opportunity to mix with the richest of the rich and the poorest of the poor. I captured some of that life in a book I wrote called *The Mosaic,* and when I finished writing it, it told me to go out on the road like Moe, the main character, did and listen to people.

Forty-five days before my trip across America, where forty-eight locations had already set up talks for me, COVID-19 came.

So, I started to look for other ways that I could listen to people. I started a show called *50 Conversations with 50 Strangers* and that was so popular it couldn't be called that anymore because 250 people responded, and while I was in the midst of that, someone said to me, 'You should be on Clubhouse,' but I had no idea what Clubhouse was.

I hesitated a little bit, as I'm an older man, and not quick to go to these new apps and new things. But the moment I got on, I realised it was exactly what I wanted to do. There's a hallway, and off of that hallway are rooms. You can go into any room and you can hear what the people in that room are thinking, feeling and saying.

In my first days on, it was really easy because nobody had any idea who I was. Nobody still has any idea who I am, but I could go into those rooms and be innocuous. I could go in and just listen. I could go into rooms where they were talking about hate and I could go into rooms where they were talking about love. I could go into rooms where they were talking about counterculture.

I just loved listening to people. And in that process, I became enamoured. I just wanted to be in that hallway all the time. I wanted to be in those rooms. I wanted to see who was speaking and I wanted to listen to them. It became a little bit addictive. I started my own room because I wanted to have a room where I could hear people speaking about the things I am interested in, and knowing what they think about. So that's sort of how it happened.

WHAT IS YOUR STORY?

I always wish I grew up and went into my dad's business, four blocks away from my parents' house, and that I had stayed with the same friends I met when I was a kid. But unfortunately, that wasn't the life I was given. My parents passed away two years apart on the same day, and that really propelled everything in my life.

I wanted to know how it was possible that my heroes could pass away and what was the meaning of life? I wanted to know what was the purpose of life and to really get a good understanding of what it is … and I don't mean this in a professional way. My book, *The Mosaic,* is a fable version of my story. It's the story of a boy in search of the meaning of life. That was me.

I had the opportunity to run a billion-dollar corporation. I walked away from it. I had the opportunity to mentor and be the co-founder with the man who founded organisational psychology, the whole movement. He was my mentor at school, and he said, 'I want you to be with me and do this with me.' I walked away from it. I had the opportunity to be a rabbi. I left one day before being ordained a rabbi in Jerusalem, Israel. I walked away from it. I had the opportunity to live in a monastery and be a monk. I spent ten years there and then I walked away from it. And so, what I've found is that I've walked away from the things most people run towards and it takes a lot of courage.

What I found is that there was something that was driving me in life that was more important than what was driving most people, not that what they're driven by isn't important, but what I was driven by wasn't what they were driven by. I found I always walked away from the place where 99% of people were running towards.

I always felt lonely and isolated, until I started to get called in to companies where people were wanting to innovate, and they were lost. They didn't have any idea how to get out of the shell of what they were doing, and they said, 'The way you're living your life, we want to know how it is that you do that. Because you are not living by the rules we live by, and we want to see the world that you see, because we believe that's where innovation lies.'

So finally, after all these years of isolation, watching these peopole who believed in things I didn't even know how to believe in, and knowing how far away from them I felt, they invited me in and allowed us to come together. What I realised is there's a beauty in the unlike-minded community, because that's where innovation happens.

WHAT HAS CLUBHOUSE DONE FOR YOU OR OTHERS?

In a world where COVID-19 doesn't let us go outside, it's allowed me to sit in my chair and see the whole world outside of me by just going into hundreds of different rooms, with hundreds of different points of view, with people that are in the midst of all sorts of things. It's allowed me to test concepts. I would go into rooms where people were yelling and fighting with each other and I would just take a moment. I had nothing to lose. Nobody knew me.

Then I would say, 'Hey, can I say something?' And I watched how when I spoke, somehow, the whole feeling of the room changed. So if we can have an impact in a room that doesn't exist, with people we don't even know, then, my God, what impact can we have in the world that does exist?

Clubhouse rooms are virtual rooms; there are no borders, there's no door that you have to go through to get there. There's a virtual door off a virtual hallway, off a virtual app. We're talking with strangers about things that are so intimate and so personal and so real. There are some rooms where people are talking about how you make money and those are great, but there are also rooms where we literally talk about the wellbeing of a human being, and how when we're able to listen to the world and the way things happen around us, how that has the ability to change the quality of the world we live in and the experience of the world we're in. So, I love it. I mean, it's a gift from heaven. And you can be in your pyjamas or a suit and tie if you want - it doesn't matter.

There's something about the voice that literally tells people who we are. And with Clubhouse being only a voice app, it's beautiful that way.

WHAT DOES YOUR FUTURE LOOK LIKE BECAUSE OF CLUBHOUSE?
I will watch and see. I mean, the beauty of life is that every moment has significance. I can only see it getting better if it continues in the way it's continuing, and we all grow together. What I would love to do, is to invite the experience of Clubhouse to become the experience of *our* house. To be able to take what we're learning in these rooms and bring it out into the world at large. The world at large is in desperate need of what's happening in these rooms.

We did a room this morning, which was absolutely beautiful. It was on finding your life purpose. There were people of every nationality, every colour, every race, every age, and we sat together and listened to each other, and we felt moved by each other. To me, Clubhouse is like the United Nations, but with real people, not delegates, and the United Nations are coming together in this virtual room, sharing and being considerate and kind to each other. Yeah, we have the trolls that come in every once in a while and disrupt, but it's okay, they're just trolls and we come back to where we are.

So, for anyone who believes that the world is a place that doesn't get along with each other, come into Clubhouse and you'll see that's just not true.

For me, it's really beautiful. It's the place to listen to other people. The rooms are set up where you come into a room and you have to listen to other people before you get a chance to speak. It's just set up that way.

Clubhouse forces listening, which couldn't be more beautiful to practice than anything because that's the practice I believe is needed to be initiated into the world. Just listen to where people are and take a chance to hear and learn, rather than speak, as you already know what you think.

What I've found in the rooms we run, which are starting to get more and more successful, is that we're less concerned with what you do. We don't care how many clients you have, we want to know who you are. Let us have the opportunity to just experience you, fall in love with you, so that by our very nature, all we want to do is find out more about you and how we can be more a part of you.

When you do that, people will come to you and want to work with you. People will come to you and ask, 'how can we do something together?' And I've found so many opportunities are opening because people just like the person that I appear to be - when they meet me, that's another story, they have to get through that, but so far, so good. And so, I would say, come into Clubhouse not wanting anything. Just come in listening and see how you can contribute.

And when your contribution is of value, people will notice you. Pete and I met on Clubhouse. I am so thankful for that moment, because I met a beautiful man who will be a lifelong friend. Those are the things I think are the benefits of Clubhouse. Beautiful things and opportunities are coming. There was a woman in the room today who's setting up a new platform to help dreamers get their dreams fulfilled. I'll be a part of that with her.

There are other people who heard me speak and they said, 'I have to do something with you.' They read my book, *The Mosaic*, and we're creating an NFT together. We got from that an artist and a musician and my wife is going to do energy healing and we're going to create, for the first time ever, a convergence of publishing, music, art and healing, so that everybody who knows this NFT will feel something from it – based on the story of humanity.

I love it. I can't recommend it highly enough.

Ram Castillo
@thegiantthinker

⚡ I help business owners get unstuck | ◎ Business Coach, Advisor, Investor | 🌏 Aussie Design Director | 🔵 Human-centred Design & CX | 💬 Creative Strategy | 🖥 Digital marketing & Branding | 📚 2x Author | 🎙 Podcaster (#3 iTunes & 250K active listeners | 🔊 Speaker (65+ events globally) | 📸 65K+ Instagram | 👥 Entrepreneur | 🎾 Amateur tennis player | 📍 Sydney, Australia | 🇵🇭 Filipino-Australian

WHY ARE YOU ON CLUBHOUSE?

I discovered Clubhouse on 15 January 2021, when more of my fellow Australian friends started to onboard. I've only been on it for two months, and it's right in the ballpark of what I love. I couldn't really get on with TikTok personally; never say never, but it's not really my thing. I do a lot of podcasting and I love having meaningful conversations so Clubhouse is perfect for that.

In terms of meaningful conversation, I'd break it down into four things; to serve and help others, to learn, to laugh, and to be vulnerable. Some of the rooms are highly entertaining too.

Another reason I'm on Clubhouse is the like-minded community. I'm a big believer in the Jim Rohn quote, 'We are the average of the five people we spend the most time with.' I wrote my second book on how to get a mentor so I'm a massive advocate for the power of having access to people who can help us cut the guesswork and see the blindspots.

I've also found that Clubhouse organically offers opportunities for collaborative partnerships. As many might have experienced; if you want to go fast, run alone, but if you want to go far, go with a team. There's so much more we can do together with partnerships. I'm seeing new economies being created, for instance, there's a rapper, partnering with an NFT artist and someone in the world of business. They're all coming together and creating innovations and opportunities in a whole new direction than that of their solo individual pursuits.

WHAT IS YOUR STORY?

My story begins before me. I'm from Sydney, originally from the Philippines, born in Manilla, but came to Australia when I was a one-year-old baby. My dad is one of eleven, and my mum is one of five. For me, I grew up knowing that I could've had a totally different life; one that potentially wasn't as prosperous.

I could have been a Filipino boy like my dad, where the only food they had some days was a tablespoon of peanut butter and some bread to share – that was their life. Mind you, he grew up with his father having passed away when he was three, so he had to be the man of the house from childhood. His mum also passed away when he was in university, when he was about eighteen.

I would ask him things like, 'How did you cope with that?' And he would say, 'We just got on with it because we didn't have the time or the luxury to grieve, we just had to keep going.' The life my parents had was about survival, and he really had to hustle to get an education to get himself out of poverty.

He graduated in marine transportation and mechanical engineering, but even though he graduated from one of the top universities in the Philippines, sadly his qualifications weren't recognised when he got Australia. He had to work in a factory to feed and house a family of three kids when migrating to Australia and not knowing anyone. That's just my dad's story.

Mum, on the other hand, had a father that wasn't really around, as he was in the military. When he was around, he would often drink which influenced flairs of abusive behaviour and womanising. My grandma (my mum's mum), had a little corner store and a sewing machine to make do and feed her five kids.

This is all context for the lens with which I view the world. For me, leading with generosity and following with care is my 'why.' I believe if you put people over profit, the money does come. I'm all about being an entrepreneur and finding ways to monetise because you do need the money in order to make an impact. It was Simon Sinek who said it best: 'A car doesn't exist so that you can fill it with fuel, it needs fuel to run, but it only exists to take you to a destination.' It's the same for business. It needs money to run, but it's not the purpose of the business. The purpose of the business is to meet a vision and to move humanity forward in some way, shape or form. That's the reason why a business or an organisation exists. That really resonates with me and is something I can connect with.

I've spent sixteen years in the in the world of human-centred design, creative strategy, and digital marketing. I started at Ogilvy in 2005, sixteen years ago, and worked my way up in that big ad-land, big communications company world. My last role was head of digital design at Mercer Bell and Saatchi & Saatchi, servicing clients like Amex, Qantas and Toyota to build digital solutions for them and customer journeys that support their business.

Previous to that, I was design director at DDB, so I worked with clients like McDonald's, and contributed to the touch screen experience for them, right across Australia. Other clients include Woolworths and Audi.

Now I'm in the space of business coaching and advisory, which I really enjoy. Taking all that enterprise-level thinking and methodologies and applying that to small to medium-sized organisations.

WHAT HAS CLUBHOUSE DONE FOR YOU OR OTHERS?
I feel it's definitely made the world smaller; if it wasn't before, it definitely is now. It's also come at the right time. Pre-COVID, I would spend three months of my year travelling the world, and speaking at events, and we currently can't easily do that due to border closures and regulations. I believe Clubhouse has not only given us access to people, but more importantly, instantaneous connection to each other and brought back a sense of humanity. Because it's a voice medium, we engage primarily with what we hear, rather than heavy visuals, videos and images. It's subtle, but the tone of a person's voice is what you interact with. With that, we feel a sense of togetherness in a world where so many are physically alone. So mental health and wellbeing is a big part of this. It's giving people hope.

I spoke to a lady recently who said she was so lonely before Clubhouse. She lives in the middle of nowhere and had no interaction, but now she can turn on her phone and have hundreds of friends. So there's a lot of mental health support and wellbeing, which I'm hugely passionate about. I want more voices at the decision-making table. I believe there's a difference between lived experience and observed experience. And if real change is to occur, we need to bring diversity of thoughts and perspectives.

And Clubhouse is doing that, bringing access to diverse perspectives, and solutions at speed. You know, good old Q&A. People are getting their questions answered with empathy and reliability through storytelling. There's a big role in the storytelling. People get insights and they connect with others in that sense. For me, Clubhouse has created new friends, new partnerships and new clients for my coaching and advisory business.

WHAT DOES YOUR FUTURE LOOK LIKE BECAUSE OF CLUBHOUSE?
I'm committed to spending more time on it intentionally, because I believe that's where global attention is potentially moving towards. I'm big on being curious on the alignment of where that attention is because digital marketing is a big part of what I do, and it's critical to test things before I potentially advise others.

I've only been on it for two months, but it feels like I've been on there for ages. The future for me is that I will be spending a lot of time on it. I don't imagine life without it. If I'm being honest, it's now a core part of my daily process, and I'm going to definitely continue to integrate it into my life for at the very least; data and insight collection.

1. Craft a very clear and succinct one-line proposition in your bio. No one gave us a handbook necessarily, especially if you're an early adopter, but having a one-line proposition should effectively, at the very least, give a sense of why people should connect with you. At the end of the day, people are asking, even subconsciously, what's in it for me? And I'm talking about the first line, because for those of you that are not on it yet, you will know that when you do get on, it's only the first one or two lines that people can see. And then if they want to, they have to click to see your whole bio. So fill out your bio, but the one-liner that people see first is critical.

2. Link your Instagram. Why? Because currently there's no way to directly chat in Clubhouse. Your Clubhouse bio can connect to your Instagram. Direct messaging via Instagram is where deeper relationships are solidified.

3. Follow people that you look up to and that you resonate with. If you follow people that are not in alignment with you, you're likely to get into weird rooms that you're not interested in. This also curates the 'rooms' you see.

4. Lead with listening rather than talking. Just because we can grab a megaphone yelling our message around, often it's best to listen. Something I learnt from a gentleman I interviewed named Oscar Trimboli here in Australia on my podcast *Giant Thinkers*, who specialises in deep listening and coaches leaders all over the world, including executives of Google and Microsoft and other large companies. He said the most critical skill in communication is listening. And the first part of listening is asking yourself, 'Are we prepared to listen?' So listening is a big part of what is needed more from an etiquette point of view as well. So listen and then speak if you feel that you can contribute to the conversation.

5. Know what it is you want to get out of Clubhouse. Otherwise it can become just another thing that sucks your time and you get caught in a rabbit hole with lack of purpose. So be clear what you want to get out of it. And once you have a clear knowing, reflect again on your bio. So if you're looking for something in particular, like investment, then say, 'I'm looking for investment,' just put it there because you're going to bump into people that can help you with that. Clubhouse is a brilliant resource that connects people lightning fast.

Lynsey Terharne
@lynseysuzanne

🏋️ Online personal trainer | 🙆 Helping women to become strong, empowered, body confident and the very best version of themselves | 💡 Co-founder of the online fitness platform – Fitness in 15 | 💪 Specialises in strength and resistance based training for body sculpting, fat loss and muscle gain

WHY ARE YOU ON CLUBHOUSE?

I actually heard about Clubhouse a good few months before I got onto the app. I didn't jump in straight away because anyone that's online already knows how many social media platforms there are, and I felt like I really didn't need another platform, so I actually resisted for a good few months. And then I was sort of pushed on it by someone else I know in the fitness industry who said, 'You've got to get on this app. It's the next big thing.' So I begged for an invite because they were really hard to come by.

And I found myself on this audio-only app with no clue what I was going to do with it, I think, maybe about mid-February. I was quite late to the game, as there were a lot of people in the UK already on it from about the end of December or January. I felt like I was behind the crowd and I started by just sitting in rooms and listening, trying to work out what it was I was going to do in there, and how I was going to use it from a fitness perspective.

WHAT IS YOUR STORY?

I'm known as Lynsey Suzanne on my social media platforms and I live in the UK in sunny Dorset. I'm in the fitness industry and an online personal trainer. I used to be face to face but due to the pandemic, I pivoted the business to be mostly online. I've been in the fitness space now since 2013.

I used to be a competitive ballroom and Latin dancer, so I was naturally quite active, but I wasn't necessarily the most sporty. I think I recall faking injuries quite a bit to get out of sports day when I was younger. I stopped dancing as I reached adulthood and began to pursue a career. When I moved to the city I just wasn't as active as I used to be.

In the country I used to walk a lot; my mum didn't drive, so we used to walk everywhere, and then suddenly I was in the city where everything was literally at the touch of a button. I didn't need to travel to get anything, really, and I discovered all the finer things in life, like eating good food, drinking and being very busy. I gained quite a lot of weight during my time working at an investment bank and it was very stressful, really long hours.

I was there when we went through one of the recessions as well, so it was a really intense time. I remember waking up one day thinking, 'I've got no zest for this at all.' The money was great, but I just had no desire to wake up and do it. It wasn't exciting. Talking about work with my mates in the pub was just boring. They didn't get what I did either.

I literally woke up one day and left. I've been pursuing a career as a self-employed person ever since and have been in fitness since

2013. I actually fell into fitness as a hobby before I went into it as a career. I remember reading a magazine one day and thinking, 'This woman looks great.' I wanted to look like her so I Googled about what she was doing and her weight training regime.

I started weight training myself, having no clue what I was doing. I literally did everything by myself, making every single mistake I could possibly make. And then over time, I realised there was a gap in the market where I could teach it rather than just navigating my way around it alone. So, I ended up competing in bodybuilding because I think the competitive nature I had when I was a kid got the better of me.

And then, of course, people comment, 'You look great. How did you do that?' So I qualified as a personal trainer and about six or seven years on, I now specialise in getting women into the weight training section at the gym. That's kind of how I got from A to B with maybe a few other steps in between.

WHAT HAS CLUBHOUSE DONE FOR YOU OR OTHERS?

Clubhouse has been like a fast forward roller coaster. It's an incredible app. It has opened my eyes to so many more opportunities than I would ever have thought possible for me, and also for business and just for networking with people as well. I came onto the app not having a clue what I was really going to do as a fitness instructor or how to utilise an audio-only app.

I've actually started a business called Fitness in 15, which initially was just an idea to try and promote myself on the app. It's now transcended into a platform; we've got investors, I've got a business partner, and this is all in the space of two-and-a-half months.

This app, for me, has opened my eyes to bigger prospects, which has been good because I've definitely got a ceiling on myself. It's been great in that perspective. It's also been really good for me to upskill myself without having to put a lot of financial backing behind myself. So many people are offering free advice. Whether you want to learn how to use LinkedIn or if you want to learn how to build funnels, there are rooms for everybody.

Not only has it been great for my own personal and business development, but also from a networking connections point of view. I am networking with people I would never in a million years be in front of, let alone have conversations with, and taking those connections offline as well. For me, it's been on this all-round app that I've managed to tick so many different boxes.

I couldn't imagine Clubhouse not being in my life anymore. If someone said to me I would lose Instagram tomorrow, sure, my business would be impacted, but I think I would get over it. Whereas with Clubhouse, I think I would be really, really sad. It's definitely been a game changer in terms of business and personal development, and it's been life-changing in terms of connections and friendships I have built as well.

WHAT DOES YOUR FUTURE LOOK LIKE BECAUSE OF CLUBHOUSE?
Well, I'd like to be in for the long game. I know a lot of people like to dip their toe in and see if it works and dip out, whereas I can see this is a social media platform where I think I will stick around for a long time. I think it's going to go through some peaks and troughs and we've seen a couple already. For me, it's been a great lead-generator for Fitness in 15. No matter whether Clubhouse disappears tomorrow, my business has been founded

on Clubhouse so it means a lot to me. I feel like I need to at least see it out and I'll probably evolve, as Clubhouse does, with new features coming out all the time.

For me, I think the future for Clubhouse is probably really strategising it into my business day and seeing it as part of my day-to-day activities. I don't see it as a social activity at all. I don't use any social media in terms of the word social, it's all strategic, 'How is this serving me as a business?'

I'm going to continue to use it like that and to build my network and grow for as long as Clubhouse is around; fingers crossed - for a long time.

CLUBHOUSE TOP TIPS

1. Show up consistently - and it doesn't matter what your consistent looks like. If you can only commit two hours a week, then that's fine, but just make sure it's consistent so that people will expect you there and people will know who you are.

2. Be very clear on why you are using the app - whether that be to listen or to add value and make sure the value you add is something you really believe in, trust in, and own. Don't add value for the sake of just speaking. If it's not true or you're not entirely sure then accept that it's a time to just listen.

3. Be mindful and open to all the opportunities available on the app - have a look around. Connect with people that maybe you're not normally in connection with off the app. There are so many different people using Clubhouse, you never quite know how they can help you out; maybe not immediately, but later down the line. Take those connections offline so that you've got them in the bank if you need them at any point.

4. Take your time with it - I think we all jumped on and probably had a bit of a honeymoon period with the app, shall we say. And then we also needed to take a bit of a step back. If you can strategise how you use it, you will benefit from it. I know it's easy to want to go all-in when you first jump in this sort of app, but you can burn out on it quite quickly. So take your time, and be strategic with it.

5. Enjoy it - If you're in a room and you don't enjoy being there, then leave; there are other rooms. You don't have to go with the crowd. If you want to break away from the normal network you are in and start looking in other rooms, it's like a parallel universe, there is so much on there. So, yeah, enjoy it, that's what it's there for, but be strategic with it because you can waste a lot of time.

Gary Doherty
@garydoherty

💡Entrepreneur & Creator of a very exclusive INNER CIRCLE | 💛 Founder of THINK Network - Europe's fastest growing independent empowerment platform. | ✖ TEDx Speaker & Organiser

WHY ARE YOU ON CLUBHOUSE?

I was introduced to Clubhouse by Pete Cohen. It came onto my radar like a bolt from the blue; it came absolutely out of nowhere.

From recollection, I was seeing people I'm connected with talking at length about this modern phenomenon – this new chat room that people were connecting on. I am usually a quick mover to change and adopt new things, but there have been one or two instances where I didn't, and then looking back, I wished I had, I actually remember thinking 'not this time,' so I was straight onto it and embraced it, and I still love it!

WHAT IS YOUR STORY?

Today, I'm a CEO and founder of a network which is Europe's fastest growing independent empowerment platform. We incorporate everything from accountability groups to mastermind public speaking coaches and webinars, empowerment shows, membership sites; the sky's the limit. I'm also the TedX Londonderry license holder.

I reside in Derry in Northern Ireland and I'm very proud to do so. I'm forty-four years old, married, a father of three, and a grand-father to two beautiful grandsons. I would say I am a person who has flourished later in life.

I have been involved in sales, management and retail for a large part of my working career, but I developed my maturity and courage to speak more and do more in my late thirties. I've always had an entrepreneurial and inquisitive mindset, searching for and creating opportunities and, I suppose for the last two years, I have really found my purpose and passion in life.

WHAT HAS CLUBHOUSE DONE FOR YOU OR OTHERS?

The first thing that jumps to mind is that Clubhouse has increased my personal brand. Twentyfold. No, that's not true, that's too small a number. My personal brand has gone through the roof, blown the roof off in fact. My Instagram handle that people can click on through Clubhouse has gone crazy.

Clubhouse has massively increased my opportunities for collaboration. I feel like I have 'early adopter' and first mover advantages on a fairly level playing field. Getting into the rooms and becoming the moderator by being seen in rooms, I am continually being respected, recognised and invited to amazing opportunities.

WHAT DOES YOUR FUTURE LOOK LIKE BECAUSE OF CLUBHOUSE?

I intend to utilise Clubhouse for the significant foreseeable future. I am enjoying my 'social butterfly' role. I am very involved in conversation, very active in the rooms and putting my hand up to speak, which grew my following organically. However, I have no real strategy, end goal or objective.

The future, for me, looks much more like embracing Clubhouse with a more defined purpose; with a career aim, objective, and goal. I am looking at my outcomes in a far more strategic way.

CLUBHOUSE TOP TIPS

1. Get your profile and picture to stand out in the room. Get the fundamentals right, don't worry about high-end strategy and what you should be doing. You'll see all different coloured backgrounds and people's profile pictures on Clubhouse; orange, yellow, blue, whatever. That's something that's very basic, but to stand out in a room firstly make sure your profile picture is professional.

2. Make sure your bio reflects the message that you actually want to give out. What is it you want to convey? What is it you want to communicate? Are you just there to talk? Are you on there to highlight your services? Are you going there to highlight your expertise? Are you on there to offer value? What exactly are you offering? And can your offer be in the first three lines of your bio? It's like a TED talk title - if you can't say it in under ten words, then it's not a TED talk. Make sure your bio's message is sharp and punchy and that people know who you are straight away.

3. Make sure your social media handles are on your profile. If they're not, I'm unfollowing you, because I'm not just there to collect followers on Clubhouse, I'm there to build relationships of purpose outside of Clubhouse. I can only do that if you've got a social media handle on your bio that I can follow. But more importantly, I can connect with you. I want to know more about what you're doing, if you're available to chat and offer to build a relationship.

Becky Duncan
@beckyduncan

🐚 Bestselling Author | Motivational entreprenuer | 🤖 The Cyber Self-Defence Coach | ⚠️ Survivor of a vicious cyber-attack | ⭐ Founder of the largest Kids Slumber and Picnic Party Styling Franchise in the Southern Hemisphere. | 📺 Featured on prime time tv: A Current Affair (Australia), Campbell Live (NZ), That's Life! (magazine), Stuff.co.nz, NZ Herald, NewstalkZB, RadioLive and Radio New Zealand, amongst other media

WHY ARE YOU ON CLUBHOUSE?

I'm from Nelson, New Zealand, and we're very lucky to not have COVID-19 on our shores at the moment, so we live quite freely, unlike many other places in the world. I joined Clubhouse because even though we're 'open,' I wanted that global connection.

I love the idea of voice to voice connection with people, like you're talking on the phone with someone and other social media sites don't have that. It's very structured and professional. With other platforms, when you post something online, you don't necessarily know if it's their true authentic self or not, because they could have spent hours crafting whatever they want to portray about themselves, whereas with Clubhouse, it's raw and authentic.

I actually begged someone to give me an invite. I was on Facebook, and asked if anyone could send me an invite to Clubhouse. I eventually found someone that did, and that's how I got in. It's a great way to connect with people in a very authentic manner.

WHAT IS YOUR STORY?

Well, I'm a survivor of horrific cyberbullying incidents which started with one man online and ended up being hundreds of men when he listed my details on a Turkish hacking website. Suddenly, I had hundreds of men after me, and he went for me in every way imaginable; he went for my career, my friendships, trying to isolate me from everybody by making things up, as well as stealing my identity.

He set up sexually derogative pages in my name. And then when all the other men came, they started hacking into my websites. They all tried to bring me down. And for a while, it worked. For seven years I went into hiding, I changed my name. I'm still an entrepreneur at heart, so when I created businesses, I always hid behind the company brand.

So, now I'm back. I have a mission. I'm armed and I've reinvented myself as the Cyber Self-defence coach. My number one mission is to stop people who incite violence against women online. My number two mission is to give all women online the tools to be able to protect themselves and have an amazing online experience, where they feel in control and safe doing it.

WHAT HAS CLUBHOUSE DONE FOR YOU OR OTHERS?

I came on to Clubhouse for the authenticity, but I wasn't prepared for all the offers of help and that shocked me. To me, especially in the current global situation, it seems whether for political or other reasons, everyone seems to be very aggro; it's like we're all divided into sections. But on Clubhouse it's not like that. From the moment I arrived, people have been wanting to help.

Pete Cohen was one of the first people I ran into and it was like, 'He's actually asking for real, he actually wants to help.' And I've seen on Clubhouse an outpouring of people who genuinely and authentically want to help each other; to build other people up and help them succeed, whatever they are doing. So Clubhouse has opened up many doors for me.

I'm talking to a big name from a global women's magazine, and she's doing an article on me. Thanks to Pete bringing me up on stage in a very large room to talk about the issues of cyberbullying. She was also on stage and heard my story. She reached out and said, 'I'd love to do a story on you.' Since then, I've had so many other offers of help, from just about everyone, it doesn't matter if they're like really big influencers or whatever.

I've also had help from other entrepreneurs trying to build their own businesses that have offered to spend time helping me as well. And I appreciate them just as much. It's not always about the big influencers that have amazing, wonderful careers and big followings and all that, it's about genuine authenticity and wanting to reach out like Pete did, and say, 'How can I help?'

WHAT DOES YOUR FUTURE LOOK LIKE BECAUSE OF CLUBHOUSE?
The Clubhouse platform is such an amazing opportunity to share our stories, to spread our messages, to make an impact on individual people. When we talk up on stage, when we're moderating or even just when we're in a room putting our hands up to ask a question, we can give our opinion on things.

But the future of Clubhouse power goes way beyond Clubhouse because people are connecting on Instagram, Twitter and LinkedIn, outside of Clubhouse. That is what's really exciting about it, unlike Facebook that wants to keep everyone in one place. I'm sure Clubhouse would love that too, but they've given us the opportunity to connect outside of the platform. I think that's really important in today's world, because the more we connect outside of one vehicle, the more authentic we will be.

We get to see people in a different light and really get to know them. That is the most amazing part about it. It's not only creating those authentic relationships within Clubhouse, but it's actually spreading those relationships in the real world, which I think is something that no other social media platform has done yet.

For me, and the world of cyberbullying, it's about creating awareness. A lot of people who haven't experienced cyberbullying don't understand the brutal and long-term impact it can have. Clubhouse has been an amazing platform for building that awareness. I've also found on Clubhouse, that when I share my story, there are people that reach out to me and say, 'Hey, I'm going through that now, can you help?'

So, it's given me an opportunity to give back and to help those people by sharing my story, just by saying, 'Hey, I've been there, I've done this. This is what happened to me.' People are feeling free and safe coming to me with their own stories and issues.

But, you know, I'm just new at this, relaunching myself as the Cyber Self-defence coach, so I'm right at the first rung of my career. I've had help from people on Clubhouse to construct my story, my bio and intro. I've had others help me on social media and I've had people that have added to my story. My story is so beautifully aligned with others that we're going to collaborate as well, which is fantastic.

1. Be Authentic. You've got to make sure you go into Clubhouse being authentic if you want to get authenticity back. What I mean by that is, don't just go into Clubhouse to see the big people and think, 'I can connect to them and sell them my stuff.' Go into Clubhouse to get to know the people, the moderators and the speakers in the rooms. Send them messages about what resonated with you and how that helped. And if you truly want to create a relationship, you need to continue it on because that one message is unlikely to be enough to develop real, authentic relationships. If they realise you are authentic with what you are doing, they'll start talking back to you, which is what happened to me.

2. Explore different rooms. Don't just stick to your own rooms or what you think you're interested in, go exploring, go into other rooms, because you meet so many different people. And variety is the spice of life. If you only ever stick to your own area, you're never going to really experience the true difference that's out there in the world.

3. Have a great profile. Make sure you've got a great profile that really reflects you, who you are and what your mission is, because that's the first thing anyone is going to see when they look at your profile. And that might help you get up on stage faster or it might help them to connect and follow you and possibly continue a relationship outside of Clubhouse.

4. Don't just be a spectator. Get involved, set up rooms, speak your truth, and use your voice, because your voice is necessary and the world needs it. Even if you're a little bit uncomfortable with it, speak up, get used to moderating and talk about different subjects. If you are hosting a room, allow people to come in and talk and share their stories.

5. Set some boundaries around the time you spend on Clubhouse. I must admit, the first couple of weeks I was on there all the time to all hours of the morning because it was so addictive. Then after the first couple of weeks, I thought, 'Hang on, I've still got a lot of work to do!' So I decided to set some boundaries, and it also means that when I'm on Clubhouse, I'm truly present. I'm able to listen to the conversations, and that then leads to authentic relationships and more opportunities opening up.

Paul Abercrombie
@paulabercrombie

🚀 Entrepreneur | 💡 Mentor | 🎙 Podcaster | Helping Entrepreneurs & Business Owners Achieve Success 📈 | ⏳ Over 15 Years in Business | 🚀 From Bankruptcy to £26m in Revenue in 18 Months | 🌍 Built 12 Companies across four countries | 📈 Barclay's fastest growing business 2016, 2017 | 😅 Made many mistakes and still learning!

WHY ARE YOU ON CLUBHOUSE?

I woke up on 26 December 2020, and my good friend Michael, a finance broker, had sent me a WhatsApp saying, 'You've got to come onto Clubhouse – you'll love it.' And then there was an invitation to join.

WHAT IS YOUR STORY?

I live in Essex, but I'm a kid from a council estate in East London where I grew up. Having dyslexia, I went through school wearing one green lens and one red lens because the doctors at the time didn't quite understand dyslexia and they thought it would help! So, I didn't get bullied … ha … honest.

Growing up, I thought I was always destined to go into a military career, but instead I took a different disciplined route and joined the London Fire Brigade after I finished school at nineteen. I was in the fire brigade for just under ten years, and left, I guess, to follow my dreams and start my own business.

Since then, I've been involved in twelve businesses, probably half of which have failed, and half of which have been successful. I'm now on a mission to help as many entrepreneurs as I can avoid the mistakes I've made over the last fifteen years that I've been in business.

WHAT HAS CLUBHOUSE DONE FOR YOU OR OTHERS?

Clubhouse has taken me back to a world of networking. I think the old-school approach to networking, you know, when years ago we used to go to the BNI breakfast meetings, and you'd really make some great connections.

I'd lost that world. I think I was in a world of semi-retirement and I guess in need of finding Clubhouse, or Clubhouse finding me. It opened my eyes to connecting with people who generally I wouldn't have connected with. If I wasn't on Clubhouse there would be no way I would be having the conversations I've had with the many people I've met in the last three months.

It got me out of a space of being confined to my home office and what was going on at home, and opened me up to the bigger world and many more connections.

When I first went into Clubhouse, and spent a little time there, like most of us, I came off thinking, 'What the hell is this?' It seemed to consume 100% of my attention.

Along with two new partners that I met on Clubhouse, I've actually created a completely new business model that wasn't even in my thinking pre-Clubhouse. We've created a marketing agency that's focused on bringing brands into Clubhouse. We've built a great community that fits with my mission of helping as many entrepreneurs as I can. Clubhouse has given me the ability to do that en masse, really.

For many of us, Clubhouse has given us the ability to grow our personal brand in the process as well.

WHAT DOES YOUR FUTURE LOOK LIKE BECAUSE OF CLUBHOUSE?

I see Clubhouse as a media channel. I see it as an equivalent to a radio network or Netflix. The future for me is to create, curate and help others create the content that people want inside Clubhouse.

And Clubhouse gives you the ability to distribute that to a much wider audience. I see our community as being the radio station and Clubhouse as being the antenna and allowing us to broadcast to many places in the world where we wouldn't be able to do that. And there are so many people we wouldn't be able to find and help if it wasn't for Clubhouse.

CLUBHOUSE TOP TIPS

1. Become the producer, not the consumer - I think you could easily fall into a trap of losing a lot of your time by listening and consuming Clubhouse. I suggest consuming Clubhouse in small doses, in the right places, in the right type of rooms. Listen to people that you've grown to respect over time. Be careful who you listen to and then focus mainly on being the producer of the content as opposed to the consumer. I think that would really help you get out of the trap of just listening to room after room after room of everybody else's content.

2. Implement the advice that you're given - especially in the rooms that we focus on, which are very inspirational, motivational and business-led. There's so many great tips, and a lot of great advice and wisdom being shared in Clubhouse rooms, you can almost get information paralysis. You can listen to advice and tips from people, but it's the implementation that counts. I would say to anybody, even if you implement one thing every week that you learn from Clubhouse in the right rooms, you can change your life forever.

3. Don't be scared of raising your hand and contributing to the conversation regardless of how irrelevant you think your comment or contribution will be. People often feel a little bit like this when starting Clubhouse. You come into the room and see people up on the stage who have got the green moderator badge next to them, and you think they must be super important or a completely different level to you to be up there. I remember the first time I was called up as a moderator and it was my turn to speak. I was genuinely shaking and couldn't get my words out. So always be prepared to contribute and be willing to contribute to the conversation. Clubhouse works because everybody shares on there and it's an open forum for everyone. It works brilliantly like that. So always be prepared to share no matter how small you feel your contribution may be.

Coach G
@guthro

🏉 Rugby player | 🏆 Rugby World Cup winner in 2007 | 🏃 Passionate coach who is motivated to make people mentally and physically stronger | 💪 Create strong group dynamics and inspire those around me

WHY ARE YOU ON CLUBHOUSE?

Well, I've had an awesome career, and experienced and achieved great things, and now it's time for me to give back. It seems that Clubhouse is the perfect platform to do that. I'm taking a lot of what I've learnt in the elite sports world and my rugby journey and transferring those values and principles into tools that everyone can use, to develop mental resilience, chase their goals and better manage daily challenges, whether that be in their personal, professional or family life.

WHAT IS YOUR STORY?

I'm a former international rugby player. I was part of the team that won the World Cup with South Africa in 2007 and have been retired since 2017. Now I'm a coach, passionate to help rugby players all over the world to improve their performances in the scrum and on the field.

To give you some background, I grew up in a town called Paarl, and my dad was actually a football coach so I originally played football until the age of thirteen. I think the only reason I played was because I was his son; there wasn't much of a choice. But I started playing rugby by chance at my new school. The coach stopped me in the hallway and asked me to play rugby. I said, 'No, I play football,' but he said, 'No, you're playing rugby.' And that moment changed my life.

Growing up in the community in South Africa, and being a person of colour has always been a big thing. My parents experienced the era of apartheid and they've worked hard to give me opportunities to become the best I could be. For example, they sent me to a great school and that type of thing. At the age of sixteen, I knew I had something special and that I could probably go all the way.

I remember my dad asking me, 'Son, are you serious about rugby? Do you want to get somewhere?' And I was like, 'Yeah, definitely.' So every single morning at 5am, he got me up for a three-kilometre run. I would go run my three kilometres, come back, go to school, go to rugby training and dad would pick me up after school, but drop me off and make me run home - it was another seven kilometres. So I was running ten kilometres a day, at the age of sixteen. That definitely taught me work ethic.

Fast forward, I went to uni. One of my biggest regrets is that I studied law and never finished it. That's why I'm telling players to make sure they get a degree. I eventually got something beyond my name at the age of thirty-seven; I got a business diploma from business school, which I'm very proud of.

When I went into the professional game, I played for the Bulls and won three championships. This was an unbelievable experience, but there were also some key negative moments. In 2009, I was written off. I was crucified in the media and people told me I needed to stop playing rugby. It was over. I was done.

But then in 2010, I was elected Player of the Year and started every single test match with the Springboks. Although being part of the winning World Cup team in 2007 was a highlight, I didn't actually play in that game, so the stand-out year for me was 2010. Especially after the coach told me in 2009 that I would never play for the Springboks again. Coming back after that for the Super Rugby campaign in 2010, I played against France on my birthday in front of my family in Cape Town, and I scored an amazing drive. That kickstarted a lot of things which led to me playing in Toulouse.

And then, in 2014, I found myself in another negative position. I played my worst match for South Africa in Argentina. I got humiliated in the scrum. That was the end of my international career. Those key moments in my life triggered a lot of things. I missed the opportunity to play in the World Cup the following year.

Getting back from that test match to my club Toulouse, my agent was waiting for me at the airport to tell me the club wanted me to leave. For two months, I played under so much pressure. My club constantly asked me if I had found another club!

That forced me to be honest with myself. I felt alone and needed help. Everybody was expecting performance, but no tools were being provided. I knew I had a big journey ahead of me. If I didn't make massive changes it would be the end of my career. I had to do a hard reset, like an iPhone, a reboot, and start from scratch.

And I started looking for extra help, exploring different training methods. I can be strong in a scrum, increase my mobility, functional patterns, functional training, all those types of things. And then I realised I wasn't the only one experiencing this. I want to help players like me. And that's when the idea was born of becoming a scrum specialist, a front-row specialist, not just giving them the tools technical-wise, but also mentally and emotionally; a holistic approach.

I retired in 2017, and in 2018 I stumbled on Zoo high intensity, low impact training and that was a massive journey. Being a retired athlete is not easy, facing life after an elite career. You can do all the prep, pitch to people what you offer, and convince them they need to spend money working with you – but that's a different ball game. Nobody prepares you for that. We have prepared our whole life to be the ultimate athlete.

There was a massive amount of learning and facing lots of challenges. Starting my own business, I found myself in the corporate space doing team building, sharing my passion, and I realised, 'Okay, I'm more than just the scrum coach.'

In 2018, I started what we call 'November project.' It's a global movement, a free fitness session, hosted every Wednesday at 6:29am. When I started in Toulouse with another coach, we had five people and by summer 2019, we had 120 people at the workout.

I'm not a life coach. I'm just a coach. I go where I'm needed and I realise I have an ability to inspire people. And today Zoo allows me to do that. Today I have the ability to inspire people in sports, business and everyday life. All I can say is, I'm only getting started.

WHAT HAS CLUBHOUSE DONE FOR YOU OR OTHERS?

To be honest, I was never someone who was that present on social media, but since COVID-19, I've been more focused as I realise people need inspiration and motivation. People are depressed and have anxiety, and if I can have even a minor effect on getting people through it, I'll be happy.

When I went into Clubhouse, I wasn't sure what it was all about. I saw it as just another social media platform, but then I saw the audience and the buzz around it and I thought, 'Okay, let me check it out.' Then all of a sudden, boom, I was like, this is great, meeting people I've never met before. This is what I do in my online training, when I train with people there's a connection, there's a bond. It might be online, but it's real. And I felt people being true to themselves on Clubhouse, people sharing, you know, people of influence sharing what happened to them, alcoholism or drug abuse, all those types of things; people being vulnerable, people adding value by sharing.

When I listened to others talk, like Pete Cohen, I've learnt so much. All of a sudden I realised Clubhouse is amazing, and that it could be another platform for me to inspire and to share my message.

The message I live by, comes down to two things:

1. The strong must serve the weak. We need to lift each other up, not push each other down.
2. Inspire one … Inspire many. If I can inspire one person a

day, they can inspire so many more.

WHAT DOES YOUR FUTURE LOOK LIKE BECAUSE OF CLUBHOUSE?
I definitely want to host more rooms on specific topics. I'm a big advocate for mental health, but also I want to help. I want to create a unique rugby community as well, because that's important to me. That's where I'm from.

But in Clubhouse, I want to add value where it's needed, like I've currently been doing. The future for me in Clubhouse is to really connect with like-minded people and be able to collaborate. There is also a business aspect, which could be positive for all of us.

The great thing about Clubhouse is the human connection. If you look at platforms like LinkedIn and so on, which is good for business sometimes, there's no soul in it. It's just, 'I can offer you this, we can do that.' But in Clubhouse, even though we can't see each other, there is connection. You listen and you can hear the tone of a person's voice, you can hear the passion. You get to know them; you can see their profile picture. When I go into a room and I see their picture up, it makes me happy seeing people I've got to know and like. Clubhouse is forming meaningful relationships.

Let's be honest, they are all people, and not just using it purely for business. If you really open up yourself, you can learn many things that can add value to your life.

CLUBHOUSE TOP TIPS

1. Put restrictions on your time in Clubhouse. I haven't even figured that out yet, and I lose so much time on Clubhouse.

2. Clubhouse can help you develop your business. Make the right connections, meet new people and the sky's the limit.

3. Get out of your comfort zone. Share your message. Show people in Clubhouse who you are. My inbox now is so long.

4. Embrace opportunities. Clubhouse is a chance to become more visible in getting your message out there. Accept invitations to podcasts and promote who you are.

5. Use it for good! We're not here to judge who uses it and why, but use it as a fusion of inspiration and connection.

Matt Fiddes
@mattfiddes

💵 Multimillionaire by 22 yrs young | 🧘 Named one of the top 50 entrepreneurs in the UK | 😊💼 Business Mentor and top adviser to businesses who want to scale and grow their business by Franchising | 🌍 Owner of the largest martial arts franchise in the world as well as the owner of many other franchise networks and property portfolio with a combined worth of over £45 million

WHY ARE YOU ON CLUBHOUSE?

I joined Clubhouse because I was told by friends that it's the next biggest social media platform and is going to be bigger than Instagram or Facebook.

They believed it would work for me and what I do in teaching entrepreneurs how to scale and grow their business and teach financial education.

It took me a while to get going, but now I realise the massive value of it. It's been the biggest free tool to pump your Instagram. A virtual stage!

WHAT IS YOUR STORY?

I was a former adviser and bodyguard to the late pop star Michael Jackson for ten years as well as other superstars and billionaires.

I became a multimillionaire by twenty-two years young.

I was named one of the top fifty entrepreneurs in the UK.

I am a business mentor and top adviser to businesses who want to scale and grow their business by franchising.

I am the owner of the largest martial arts franchise in the world with over 1000 locations, as well as the owner of many other franchise networks and owner of a property portfolio, which is one of the biggest in the south-west of England and still growing.

WHAT HAS CLUBHOUSE DONE FOR YOU OR OTHERS?

Clubhouse has given me the ability to get back into the conference room again. When you listen to the speakers, you can get access to people like we never have before, and it's all for free as well. It's connecting like-minded people who want to work together. It's bringing people together at the right time. I do think it's going to be the next big thing. I really do. It will be interesting to see how Clubhouse will be effected when we go back to normality after the COVID-19 pandemic.

WHAT DOES YOUR FUTURE LOOK LIKE BECAUSE OF CLUBHOUSE?

Well, you can do anything on it now. I mean, if I want instructors for my organisation I can have an instructor recruitment room, you know, like an interview room. You can see there's going to be all sorts of get-togethers on there. I'll tell you the big thing I've noticed, because it's audio, successful people don't have to worry about their hair and makeup like we do when we go on TV.

The biggest thing is we now have access to the global stage, whereas before it was difficult to organise. Now we have two or three thousand people in the room and we're on stage and making some great American friends right now. It's just awesome. I'm interested to see where it goes. I have made some close friends from all around the world and reconnected with old friends I lost contact with.

CLUBHOUSE TOP TIPS

1. You need to be active. When someone starts a room, raise your hand early to get more of a chance to get on stage. You get on stage because people respect that confidence.

2. Connect on Instagram at the end of the room. You never know, it might bring you to your next business deal or next level of personal development education.

3. Don't forget about some of the smaller rooms, because they are good too. Some of the smaller ones have the best content and will help to build your following.

4. Run your own rooms on your subject. Build your own raving fans.

5. Watch out for fakes! There is a lot of people claiming to be someone they are not. Use Google to look for social proof.

Teri Healy
@terihealy

Designer of the 8 & 1/2 Minute system | 🕯 Transform your life in minutes a day | 🔹 Speaker | ⭐ Coach | 📕 Author | ✴ Visionary | ✦ My life is a story of transformation | 💛 Everything that happened has prepared me to serve others | ⭐ Committed to impacting 10 million lives

WHY ARE YOU ON CLUBHOUSE?

I found Clubhouse through a former coaching client. We were having lunch and were talking about how to get my voice out there, you know, how to get my message out into the world. She said I needed to connect with my tribe, to find people who are like-minded, and interested in the same things as me. So she said, 'Get into Clubhouse,' and she invited me in.

WHAT IS YOUR STORY?

I'm Teri Healy and I live just outside of Chicago. I'm a speaker, coach, author and visionary. My story is one of survival and transformation. When I talk about survival, it's like I defied all the odds; statistically I should have been on the street, incarcerated, addicted or dead from the history that I've had.

When I was fifteen, I was sitting in class at school and the guidance counsellor called me into his office. After I sat down, he asked me why I was going to school. I wasn't sure why he was asking, but I couldn't tell him the real answer.

The reason I went to school was so that I could eat. I lived in a county that gave me free breakfast and lunch. So, on school days I got to eat twice. The weekends were horrible for me and in the summertime when school was out, it was excruciating. I didn't have an answer for him.

He asked me if I knew that I was failing all of my classes, except for orchestra. I didn't know that, but I wasn't surprised. Then he said that he was confused because I was actually very smart. That comment put me immediately on guard. In my world, men didn't say nice things to me without an ulterior motive. As I sat there trying to figure out what I had to do to get back to class, he went on to explain.

There were papers that he took out of my file and showed me. We had done testing at the beginning of the school year that gave placement data in percentiles. In Math, I ranked ninety-fifth out of one hundred students, and in English, I ranked ninety-eighth. So he said that he was confused. Why were we sitting there talking about me failing the ninth grade when we should be talking about where I wanted to go to college.

College? I had never in my life thought about going to college. I had never even thought about graduating high school. My world was about day-to-day survival. He gave me copies of the papers and sent me back to class. Thankfully, I had the physical proof as I think that I would have talked myself out of that entire conversation without it.

As I was heading back to my class, I realized that I'd had a belief about myself that I'd never seen before. I saw that up until that moment, I believed I was mentally disabled; back in those days, we called it being mentally retarded.

I saw that I knew it wasn't a truth for me and now I had the paperwork to prove it. My entire world changed on a dime and opened up to possibilities I could never have imagined.

It's taken a lot of work and many years to be ready to bring my gifts to the world. And I know it sounds strange, but I have a really unique ability to connect with people. I can speak to any audience even if the demographic looks nothing like me. When I first started speaking, I went into one of the toughest cities for crime in the United States. I would speak in the homeless shelters and the battered women's shelters because I wanted to touch people at their deepest, darkest and most raw moments. I knew if I could get in front of those people, and could actually help them make a shift, I could bring that to anyone. That was my training ground. There's something about my voice as well, it's very soothing and calming, and once I start to speak, people are automatically connected to me.

And I know that connection comes from a shared understanding of hardship. I came through it. I get it. I feel it. And my compassion comes through. You couldn't even imagine the amount of compassion I have for other people and their stories and journeys.

WHAT HAS CLUBHOUSE DONE FOR YOU OR OTHERS?

Well, I've only been on it for maybe three weeks now, but what it's done is actually open up doors for me across the world. I have connected with so many people from London, which is interesting. I'm getting my voice out to many places, and it seems the platform is connecting me with a lot of women.

I would never have had these connections and opportunities if it wasn't for Clubhouse.

WHAT DOES YOUR FUTURE LOOK LIKE BECAUSE OF CLUBHOUSE?
Interestingly enough, connecting to Pete Cohen actually kind of triggers this and it makes me shake a little inside. I see Clubhouse as the vehicle I've been waiting for, to take me to where I've seen myself going, and ultimately to what my entire life has prepared me to do.

You just know you're in the right spot. You're right there. It's a knowing inside.

I would like to see Clubhouse become the place that starts connections. I know I'm supposed to serve others with my message, but I can't do that while reaching people one by one, like by bumping into them in the grocery store. With Clubhouse, I see things growing exponentially, which means I can serve so many others, and then they can share it, and so on and so on.

CLUBHOUSE TOP TIPS

1. Get up onto the stage and engage. The first two times I wanted to speak I was actually nervous and I didn't want to get up on stage. That was kind of interesting to me because that's what I do for a living. But I guess Clubhouse is different, because when you're speaking, you can't see your audience. For me, it's like I didn't know if I was connecting. But I encourage everyone, no matter what you're feeling, to put your hand up and just get up there. Even if it's a couple of words, you can make the connections happen when you're up there on the stage.

2. Try lots of different rooms. Don't think you're only going to want to hear from people in certain rooms. Pop in and get a feel for it, and if you don't like it, pop back out. I have found myself in some very interesting rooms that I wouldn't have thought would be interesting to me, but it's a whole new kind of conversation.

3. Connect with people on Instagram. Follow up outside of Clubhouse if you like them. If somebody moves you, send them a note, follow them, or even just message them. Let them know how you feel. This is the kind of thing that brings momentum and helps you make connections.

4. Tell anyone and everyone about Clubhouse. Sometimes we worry that it might not be their thing, but who are we to say? So I share it with everyone. Some people shut down right away but others are like, 'Can I have an invite?'

5. Don't use Clubhouse with an agenda. It's not there for you to promote yourself or to sell your goods. I know when we're there it's easy to say, 'Look at me and what I'm offering,' I get that, it's a human thing. Yes, we've all got to eat, but other people smell that and they shut down from it. Clubhouse is not the time or the place for that kind of a conversation, it's best to take that connection and interact outside of Clubhouse.

Ryan Today
@collaborating

⭐ Youth suicide survivor, addict and homeless teenager | ☀️ Now a life coach and pioneer | 🌱 Runs a startup helping people create lasting bonds with portable plants, called Air Ferns | 🎙️ Online workshop "Hum To Heal" teaches proven sound, breathing, body-mindfulness techniques

WHY ARE YOU ON CLUBHOUSE?

I was a speaker at a three-day online event, and one of the other speakers said, 'Hey, man, you've got a great voice, you should be on this app called Clubhouse.' I hadn't heard of it, but he explained it was an audio app available by invite only, and he had a couple to give. I'm all about audio, so I was intrigued, but I don't really do social media, so I left it at that.

The next day, I was in a breakout group, and someone else said the same thing, 'You should really be on this Clubhouse app!' So I circled back with him, but he had already given his invites out. I asked a few people, but no-one had invites. At this point, my intrigue had been replaced with compulsion. I felt called. Trusting my intuition, I downloaded the app, created my profile, and knew that the invitation would come at the right time.

I didn't realize it would happen so fast! I had just settled in to watch a movie with my son, when a notification on my phone popped up, 'You've been nominated by Kurt Walker. Welcome to Clubhouse.'

I clicked the button to accept and the next thing I hear is the voice of Ed Nusbaum, one of the most amazing people I've ever met, saying, 'Hi Ryan, welcome to Clubhouse!' Ed is a key figure and supporter of the local entrepreneur community that I've been blessed to know for over ten years. We hadn't chatted in a while, so it was quite a surprise to get on Clubhouse so fast and then to have Ed, right there, live in real time to welcome me. The first few minutes on the app blew me away, but the nonstop parade of amazing people and conversations has not slowed down. It feels like a lifetime's worth of connections and community has been forged in just seven short weeks.

WHAT IS YOUR STORY?

I'm Ryan Garey-Today. I'm from Arizona, originally born and raised in California, with a five-year stint in Utah. I've been in Arizona since 1998.

Curiosity and love are my two key motivators. Curiosity pulls me forward even when I don't want to, even when I don't feel like I have it in me, or I'm too hurt or too tired to move. I use curiosity to consistently pull myself forward because love of a thing or desire alone doesn't necessarily pull us forward or change us in the ways we want. Curiosity can.

I was a homeless teenager due to drug addictions and a painful auto-immune disease and was later diagnosed as bipolar with PTSD. I wanted to change and I loved my family so very much, but neither desire nor love seemed to change my circumstance. I was stuck, trapped in a pain-ridden body I didn't want to be in. With this in mind, it won't be a surprise that suicide was on the table for most of my life. Having witnessed multiple family suicides when I was younger, I tried cutting my wrist before I was ten, and still carry the scar with me.

I'm glad I didn't die. Even though I've been a motivational speaker and coach since 2002 ... 2020 was the year I finally put the nail in the coffin for suicidal ideation and am fully contracted and in love with life!

How? Leveraging the power of curiosity to pull myself forward 'just one more step,' I learned how to truly be my own boss. More specifically, my own BEST boss!

I think, with most people, when they talk about wanting to be their own boss they're really saying they don't want to work! They want freedom. They want to be in control. They don't want to be controlled. But what they don't realise is that means you've got to control yourself. You've got to boss yourself around. You've got to get yourself to do things that you don't want to do, or things you may not be capable of doing. But it doesn't matter, you've still got to do it. The job's got to get done and you've got to do it with a good attitude. And when you're done, you need to stop and look back and ask yourself, 'What could I have done better? How was that a good investment of time? What can I do to improve?' That's what good bosses do, so doing that for yourself is what it really means to be your own boss.

Even when I was selling frozen meat door to door in Arizona to get out of homelessness, I was learning to be my own boss. That's the skill set I had to learn; to boss myself around effectively in the best possible way, with love. And ultimately, that's how I got to where I am. I've increasingly been learning to live by a simple rule: if I'm not at peace with it, I don't do it. If I wouldn't expect an employee to do something they weren't at peace with, or didn't have integrity with, then why would I ask myself to do it?

Being your own boss doesn't mean you have to be self-employed, either. There are plenty of people who are employees but they are effectively their own boss. We see them at work; they don't need to be managed, or to be told what to do or directed. They're open to direction and feedback, of course, because as their own boss they are looking for ways to improve. So being your own boss does not necessarily mean you are an entrepreneur or self-employed. Similarly, there are plenty of people who are self-employed but they're not their own boss, they're still being pushed around by their clients and the world around them.

Professionally, my first job was at Walden Bookstore. I was only there for nine months of the fiscal year and was number three nationwide in the company for selling their discount reader cards, because ultimately I was just trying to serve the customer, with curiosity for their needs, not an agenda to sell.

The homelessness began after that, by choice at first, choosing to live freely in the world as a dharma bum. Eventually, freedom became my prison and I found myself a panhandling addict unable to change my circumstance.

So that's my story. I moved myself, step by curious step, out of homelessness and hopelessness and into a place of love and growth, experientially learning on a progressive basis. Basically selling myself on doing what it took to become someone new, curious as to how much I could change. I found a job selling frozen meat door to door, and like a good boss, I helped myself learn from every experience at a door and become someone greater before I got to the next. I sold my way out of homelessness and into newness.

That led me to the University of Phoenix selling online education, back in 2001, when it was still a new thing. I was blessed because it was all over the phone. People had no idea what I looked like or who I was, so I could just pretend to be a 'professional' college counsellor. That's when I started to learn to use my voice. As a matter of fact, I fought very hard to get the job. I interviewed multiple times. It took me six months. I worked with a temp agency at first just to get in with the company.

When I finally got in, I was coming home from being a college counsellor, grabbing my didgeridoo, jumping on my skateboard and hanging out with homeless kids all night, because that's who I identified with. I was using my professional development to pull my life out of the gutter, to sell myself on a different reality of who I might be, even if I didn't want to at the time.

For me, success is working with wanting. Just because I didn't want anything better at the time, doesn't necessarily mean I wouldn't want it later. Hence why I changed my name to Ryan Today, because I am both present and living for the day, but also making sacrifices so Ryan tomorrow has opportunities Ryan today doesn't.

At the University of Phoenix, I was able to hone my voice to coach others into becoming adult experiential learners; I wasn't just selling online degrees. I realised I had to develop my voice, when a sweet lady on the phone said, 'I don't mean to cut you short, but I'm trying to have a serious conversation about my career and my future, and you sound like my twelve-year-old grandson, is there someone else I can talk to?' I was devastated, but I talked my manager into buying me a cassette recorder so I could record my own voice, and listen to it on my lunch break and on the way home. And that sweet lady was right ... I just didn't have any vocal presence. I worked with my voice and adopted the mindset of a counsellor in a big leatherback chair in a room full of books. I imagined people coming into my office and asking me about their career and their life, and I was the guy who had it all figured out. I started pretending I was that counsellor, not a homeless, skateboarding, didgeridoo-playing, addict. I 'faked it' until I 'made it.' I sold my psyche on a new reality. That's how I got into coaching; I had students coming back saying they got more from working with me than they did out of school and encouraged me to look into it.

I was with the University of Phoenix for almost a decade. By the time I left, they were one of the largest educational companies, with 13,000-plus employees, a bit different from the two hundred of us working at the end of a cul-de-sac in Phoenix when I started and even earned a letter of recommendation from the CEO of Apollo Group (parent corp. of University of Phoenix) for my contribution to adult experiential learning. Being an instinctually loving person, I'm very naïve, despite being street smart. I honestly thought we were on a mission to revolutionise the way adults experienced life and learning, but it turns out we were on a 'for profit' mission, which I should have known because we were a 'for profit' university.

I left the university to go to Infusionsoft; a fledgling marketing automation company, with just eight sales reps when I joined.

After a short time, I was asked to coach the two hundred certified marketing automation coaches they had and run their partner channel. Working with curiosity and love, I ended up doubling that channel's performance the very first month in that position.

'You're not selling software, you're a marketing automation coach,' was my mantra. The next thing I know, I had gurus flying in to work with me, doing Infusionsoft implementation with clients that got me speaking on stages in front of thousands of people; speaking with guys like Tony Robbins, Michael Gerber, Dan Kennedy, John Carlton, Bob Proctor, etc. It was a lot of fun. We were a giant company two years later when I left in March 2010. I left because I recognised I was once again in a situation where our small business was becoming a corporation where the focus on sales and scalability conflicted with the curiosity, service, love-centric soul in me. I knew the only way to create the quality of work life I needed was to be self-employed.

WHAT HAS CLUBHOUSE DONE FOR YOU OR OTHERS?

For me, Clubhouse has untapped my potential in more ways than I can express. It's accelerated the ability for me to get out of my head and into my heart. It's allowed me to see and practice the art of valuable vulnerability, because lots of people are showing vulnerability and authenticity as a key part of the emerging economy.

There's a value chain that's wrapped around vulnerability. There's space just to be vulnerable and be broken down, but there's also a skill set to being simultaneously vulnerable, yet powerful. And it's an interesting dynamic that we as a society haven't really been able to play out.

Another thing it's done for me is allowed me to test, play and have fun experimenting, just being, unfolding and evolving alongside everyone else. I love them all so very much and it's clear to me now, that we are all forever evolving beings.

Ultimately, Clubhouse has cured my depressive realism. For those who don't know, depressive realism is an actual diagnosis for those who are aware enough to see how the world works, and it's depressing! And it can be depressing to me, as I've been looking at the world being run by marketers. Marketers who know it's not the best solution that sells, but the best marketed solution. It's all about appearance and posturing, not solutions and connection, to most of them. And the market is none the wiser. But Clubhouse has cured that, because if this many people are this hungry, and capable of such high-level of conversation on Clubhouse, humanity has got this! We're not doomed! Yes, we've got problems and challenges we have to work through, but humanity is evolving, and it seems like we are evolving together now. Alone, we are broke. Together, I feel hope. I feel hope for humanity and the world my children are going to grow up in.

WHAT DOES YOUR FUTURE LOOK LIKE BECAUSE OF CLUBHOUSE?
The future for me in Clubhouse continues to be collaborating at ever higher levels. It's a sacred obligation that both reveres the sovereignty of the individual as well as that individual being part of a collective and a part of the whole. So, the individual is more important than the collective and the collective is more important than the individual. How many movies are on the theme of exploring the value of one life versus the value of many? I think those movies have been begging us to address this issue personally. And I think the future of Clubhouse is us

unfolding what that looks like and learning to grapple with the issue, both inside ourselves and as a society to say, 'What is the value of my contribution?' Because I tell you, a big part of getting out of suicidal tendencies was finding a will to live above and beyond just providing for my family. It came down to a will to live, not towards a legacy in the future which is abstract, but the legacy of my presence and the presence I will have tomorrow. What am I doing today to improve my future, tomorrow?

So, when it comes down to, 'What is the future of Clubhouse?' or, 'Clubhouse is our future,' I think of when people say, 'The children are our future.' I used to think that 'the children are our future' was such an abstract concept, but think about how the conversations we are having today could impact the future. A conversation held today has the power to impact others a year from now, five years from now, ten years from now. It's possible that a ten-year-old kid, reading this conversation, could be so moved by it that five years from now, by the time they're fifteen, they've created some kind of new lifesaving procedure that saves my life, saves my kid's life, allows others to live a fuller living expression in the world.

All of these things become possibilities because of what we did today, the sacrifices made today. And so the future of the children, our future and the future of Clubhouse, isn't some abstract twenty, thirty, or fifty years off in the future, it's a month from now, a year from now, five years from now, and it comes fast! So the future Clubhouse is the art and the sacred science of collaborating, and that IS the future.

CLUBHOUSE TOP TIPS

1. Three steps: listen, serve, then share, that's the order and the pattern I've found.

2. Don't hesitate to pop in and out of rooms. It's okay to be a social butterfly, especially at first. No-one's going to be offended if you pop in and out - it's okay. It's also really important to listen to the tone of the room.

3. Not all moderators reset the rooms on a regular basis. Sometimes we start on one topic, and four hours later what we're talking about has nothing to do with where we started. Every room really is so different, so be prepared to listen. Just because someone asks you up on stage to speak does not mean you need to speak. It's okay to hit 'maybe later.' When you get up on that stage, it's important to ask, 'Who am I serving by being here?'

4. Are you there to be served, are you there to serve, or a little bit of both? At least be clear, because if you want to raise your hand and get up on stage, be clear of what you want from that. Even if it's just to say 'Hi,' and chat, that's cool. Be clear about your intent of who and how you are being served. Who is being served by you getting up on stage? Whether you raise your hand or they invite you, be clear, as sometimes they can be serving themselves by having you get up on stage.

5. Listen and take time to discover if you want to step up. Even in listening mode, who is being served by you listening? Just having your presence in the room is powerful. Everyone's presence is powerful on this app - every single one of us. So listen, find out who you're serving and that's when you can share, share your name, share what you're about, share what's appropriate and relevant to the room.

Proceeds from this book will be donated
to the following charity:

Charity Number 1138100

www.cocosfoundation.co.uk

www.ingramcontent.com/pod-product-compliance
Lightning Source LLC
Chambersburg PA
CBHW041637050326
40690CB00026B/5246